SEO DOJO

SEO DOJO

Search Engine Optimization Mastery for Martial Arts Schools

Dan Verghese

SEO Dojo: Search Engine Optimization for Martial Arts Schools

ISBN 978-1-7394268-0-4.

Disclaimer

Although the author has made every effort to ensure that the information in this book was correct at the time of publication and while this book is designed to provide accurate information in regard to the subject matter covered, the author assumes no responsibility for errors, inaccuracies, omissions, or any other inconsistencies herein and hereby disclaim any liability to any party for any loss, damage, or disruption caused by errors or omissions, whether such errors or omissions result from negligence, accident, or any other cause.

The author makes no guarantees concerning the level of success, web traffic or search rankings you may achieve by following the advice and strategies contained in this book. Rankings can go down as well as up – any changes you make are at your own risk.

To martial arts instructors and school owners everywhere. Whatever your art, may you continue to transform lives, one student at a time.

CONTENTS

APPENDICES

ACKNOWLEDGEMENTS

This book is a fusion of two key themes of my life – martial arts, and digital marketing. I'd like to thank everyone who has helped me develop as both a digital marketer and a martial artist over the last twenty-plus years. Special thanks go to Rick Dubidat and his coaching group, The Growth Network, for their invaluable support and advice on how to run and grow a successful martial arts business. Thanks also to my beta readers, Allie Somerville Hannell and Lily Dedman, for their invaluable feedback and advice on the manuscript. My final thanks go to my wife Anna, and my daughter Isabelle, for their ongoing support.

1

INTRODUCTION

What SEO is, and how this book will help you learn it.

SEO. Search Engine Optimisation. It's a simple acronym, but one that encompasses a vast array of strategies, tactics, and best practices for getting websites to rank high in search results. It is a complicated subject, but putting a little effort into the basics can go a long way, and the rewards are huge.

You may ask, why does a martial arts school owner need to worry about SEO? We can always get new students by running Facebook and Google Ads, right? Well, maybe. Martial arts marketing is ever evolving. Gone are the days where you could drop a few thousand leaflets through doors and run some public demos to fill your dojo floor with eager new students.

Marketing has gone digital, and it is ever more difficult to cut through the online noise to reach potential students or their parents. Modern life exposes us to hundreds, if not thousands, of ads every day. Think about the last time you scrolled social media. How many ads did you see? Can you remember what they were for? Probably not. Whilst digital ads are still effective and should usually form an important part of your recruitment strategy, they can be expensive and unreliable. They also rely on platforms that you do not own, which is a risk if ads are your only marketing channel.

What's more, changes in public perceptions around privacy and data-gathering have led to many people moving away from certain social media platforms, and to a tightening up of these companies' ability to track users, making re-targeted ads less effective. Lead generation via paid advertising relies on an ongoing expenditure, which may or may not bring a return on your investment. When you turn the money pump off, the well of new leads instantly dries up.

Search engine optimisation is a powerful weapon in your armoury, as there will always be a proportion of potential students and their parents actively searching for martial arts classes in their area. These are people with an obvious interest in your services, so their pump is primed. They are more likely to book trial classes, show up, and become students than somebody attracted via a Facebook ad.

These customers are looking for the best class in their local area, but the class they end up attending will almost certainly be one of the top results they see when they search. You need to make sure that's you! According to research by respected SEO guru Brian Dean[1]:

- 27.6% of all first page clicks go to the site in the top spot on Google.
- Clicks to the top-ranked page are ten times as high as that in position ten.

---

[1] Backlinko, 2022: https://backlinko.com/google-ctr-stats

- The click-through-rate for sites appearing in positions eight to ten is virtually the same. So, you need to rank higher than this to see meaningful gains.

SEO is hard, so why bother?

Competitive advantage

Most martial arts clubs are stuck in the digital stone age – their websites are poorly laid out, dated, and have little unique content. Many instructors rely on other methods for gaining students. Often their classes are small, as they put little effort into marketing. Many instructors are happy with this, and that's fine if it works for them. But if you have ambitions to grow your school or to become a full-time professional instructor, you need to aim higher.

Given that so few MA schools put any serious effort into SEO, those top spots in the search engine results pages (SERPs), are there for the taking. A little basic SEO, every now and again, can go a long way and make a measurable difference to your success.

Don't build your house on rented land

Facebook and Instagram ads can often work well for many school owners. But I often hear complaints that the leads have dried up, and that what used to work well no longer does. These platforms can change at any time, and you have no control over them. When Elon Musk bought Twitter, user sentiment and the company's prospects changed overnight. If Facebook (or your platform of choice) suspended your account overnight, what impact would this have on your business?

As with any sustainable business and marketing strategy, diversification is key. Placing more effort into the marketing assets *you own outright* is a sensible and less risky approach to long-term success. You own your website and your email list, so make the most of them. If you use a software-as-a-service website provided by a billing company, you benefit from speed and convenience, but sacrifice ownership and control. Consider whether this is a good long-term strategy for your business.

Set yourself up for long-term success

Once you optimise your website and have a sound understanding of SEO, you can rank high in search and reap the rewards from then on. It may take a few months to see results, compared to the instant gratification of paid ads, but the payoff is also longer-lived. With SEO you are investing your time, rather than your money. Clubs in their early stages that lack a significant ads budget should focus on 'organic leads' (leads that you did not have to pay to attract).

What does good look like?

Ranking high in search will attract much greater traffic than appearing outside the top-ten results. The more visitors your site receives, the more leads you will receive, provided you optimise your pages for lead generation (more on this later). For most Western countries, Google is the only game in town in today's online search environment. By following good SEO practices for Google, your site is also bound to rank higher in Bing or any other search engine popular in your country. Following the advice in this book will help you to:

- Identify **what** to rank for (your target keywords).
- Rank in your **local area** (local SEO).
- **Dominate** the top Google rankings.

Google domination

This book will teach you how to not only appear high in local search results, but how to dominate the first page. But what do we mean by domination? When it comes to ranking websites, it is not only the home page that we want to rank in position one, or at least the top three. You want to dominate as many of the top ten spots as you can, excluding your competitors and becoming the natural choice for anyone interested in martial arts classes. Potential students (or their parents) will see you everywhere and assume you must be the best or most popular choice in the area. You can achieve this through a combination of:

- A well-optimised home page.
- Pages for specific programmes and locations.
- Great content, such as blog posts.
- Active, cross-linked social media profiles.
- Backlinks and local business directory listings.

How to use this book

SEO Dojo contains a structured programme for attracting more visitors, and potential students, to your website. It begins with basic concepts before progressing to more advanced strategies, from the fundamentals of SEO and how to carry out keyword research, to more advanced techniques for backlink building and technical optimisation. I recommend reading it cover to cover so you do not miss anything, but equally you can jump around and dip into specific chapters if you already have some SEO knowledge. If you encounter any unfamiliar terms, check the glossary in Appendix IV.

This is, to the best of my knowledge and at the time of writing, the only SEO book written specifically for martial arts school owners.

Accompanying the book are some free, downloadable templates which you can access by visiting:

https://bit.ly/seo-dojo-download

2

SEO CONCEPTS

Understand the fundamentals governing effective SEO.

Search Engine Optimisation aims to get pages on your website ranking as high as possible in the SERPs. The goal is to attract as many relevant visitors to your site as possible, increasing leads or sales. When we refer to “search engines”, in most countries of the world there is only one player in town, the 'Big G' - Google. The advice in this book focuses on ranking your site well on Google, but in optimising your site according to best practices and by producing high-quality content, you will turbo-charge your positions in other search engines, such as Bing.

To generate as much business as possible through a website via organic search, there are three key objectives:

1. Rank one or more pages as high as possible for your target keywords.
2. Increase the number of relevant keywords the site ranks for.

3. Get the best possible click-through-rate (CTR) from the SERPs to the website.

Putting an SEO plan in place that systematically addresses each of these three factors will lead to increased growth for your martial arts school.

What isn't SEO?

Google ads do not fall under SEO, as you are essentially buying web traffic, as opposed to encouraging it organically. You pay for traffic to your website through text ads that appear at the top or bottom of Google's results pages. Facebook and Instagram ads are similar. PPC (pay-per-click advertising) is great for immediate traffic boosts and should certainly form a part of your marketing strategy. It works alongside SEO to drive leads to your site and can bring more immediate results. The downside to PPC is that it costs money, and you lose all benefit the moment you stop paying for traffic. SEO takes longer to show a return, but the benefits are longer lasting.

Social media is also distinct from SEO, although there is some overlap. Social is a key plank of many martial arts clubs' student acquisition strategy. You can use it to generate leads within the social platform (e.g., Facebook, Instagram), or to drive traffic to your website. Social traffic to a site is valuable and may indirectly benefit your SEO, but it is a separate channel from organic traffic. We'll look at how your social profiles can help enhance your SEO later in the book.

How search engines work

Search engines use complex algorithms to determine what results to show to a user for a given keyword search. "Ranking factors[2]" are specific aspects of your online presence that the search engine's algorithm considers when performing its calculations. Google looks at over two hundred of these, and usually only provides clues as to what they are, as their algorithm is a closely guarded secret. We can group ranking factors into some broad categories:

- Page-level ranking factors
- Site-level ranking factors
- Domain ranking factors
- Backlink ranking factors
- Brand ranking factors.

Page-level factors include metadata, headings, and the quality of page content. Site-level factors address issues including website structure, navigation, security, and trust. Backlinks refer to the number and quality of links from other domains to your domain. Brand factors may include the number of brand-name keyword searches and visibility on social media. Each of these will be addressed later in the book.

Local SEO

Local SEO is a specialised sub-discipline of search engine optimisation. It deals with searches where geographic proximity is important, like "martial arts classes near me" or

---

[2] See a detailed list of ranking factors at Backlinko: https://backlinko.com/google-ranking-factors

“aikido in Birmingham”. Google uses a separate algorithm to determine the results for local searches, when it detects that the search has local intent. This algorithm includes some extra ranking factors and weights them according to different rules.

For example, how close a business is to the searcher is one of the prime ranking factors, so Google Maps data is important for local search results. Most people use their phone to search when looking for a local business, so it is vital to consider the mobile experience your website provides. If you are building a new site or thinking about a redesign, choose a content management system (CMS) and theme/template that gives you the best combination of flexibility, speed, and mobile optimisation.

Local results also include other unique features, such as the Local Pack, a panel that appears at the top of many local search results. It displays extra information about the three most relevant results, like star ratings, reviews, physical address, and a pin on the map.

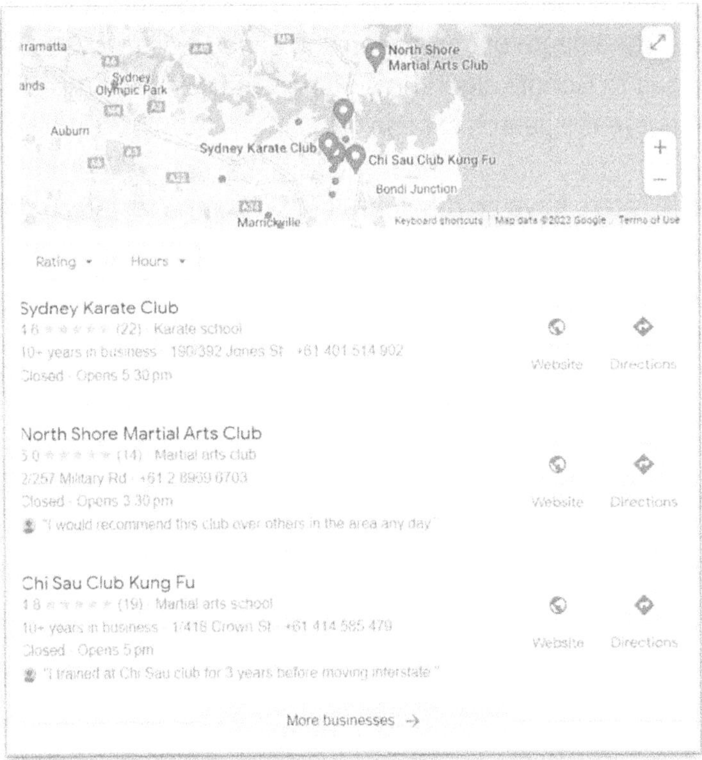

Local Pack results for "martial arts clubs in Sydney"

As martial arts schools are local businesses serving a clientele within a defined area, a rigorous approach to local SEO is crucial.

It's time to E-E-A-T

Get your fingers out of the buffet. We're not talking about food. E-E-A-T is an acronym used in Google's Search Quality Rater Guidelines, which stands for Experience, Expertise, Authoritativeness, and Trustworthiness. The Search Quality

Rater Guidelines is a reference document used by Google's crack global team of search ranking experts. They evaluate changes to Google algorithms as part of their ongoing efforts to improve the search experience.

Quality raters have no direct impact on search results, but SEO professionals pay close attention to their guidelines. They provide insight into what factors Google's algorithm values in a website, and the real business that lies behind it. The acronym used to be E-A-T, but in late 2022 Google added the second 'E', for experience.

Experience

Google is looking to rank websites for businesses that have real-world experience in their subject. For sites offering medical advice, you would expect content created by qualified doctors to outrank something written by an amateur. Likewise, would you prefer to learn about martial arts from someone who has read all the books, or someone who has trained for thirty years, won a world championship, and had a good standing in the sector? The "experience" requirement applies most stringently to sites offering high-stakes advice, such as on legal, medical, or financial issues.

Expertise

Google also wants to know that the content creator has a deep understanding of their topic, that content is accurate and comprehensive, and that the people behind the content have the appropriate experience, training, or qualifications. Consider how you can demonstrate your expertise on your site. Attribute content to an author and provide an author bio that details your expertise and relevant qualifications.

Authoritativeness

Authoritativeness is the extent to which the website is an authority on its subject. Are other authoritative sites linking back to it? Has the company received mentions and citations by other authoritative sources, and are they a well-known name in their space?

Trustworthiness

Trust is now the overriding factor within the E-E-A-T guidelines. It is central to how Google's human content raters assess the quality of search results. Without trust, a website will have poor E-E-A-T, even if its experience, expertise, and authoritativeness are on point. Trust is especially important for ecommerce sites, as they process payment information and personal customer data.

To demonstrate trust, make it obvious who wrote your content. Include reviews and testimonials. Take site security seriously, keeping your SSL certificate up to date and ensuring your shopping cart, if you run an online Pro Shop, is secure.

Action Points

- ☐ Learn the main categories of ranking factor.
- ☐ Check the Local Packs for your area's local searches.
- ☐ Familiarise yourself with E-E-A-T.

3

UNLOCK THE POWER OF KEYWORDS

Why keywords are important, and how to identify them.

Keyword research may sound boring, but it is the vital first stage of any SEO campaign (or project). We first need to know *what* terms we want to rank for before we can start thinking about *how* to do it. The market is full of fancy, paid-for keyword research tools. Most martial arts schools do not have a large marketing budget, so I'll show you how to pick the right keywords without spending money.

What do we mean by a "keyword" anyway? In SEO parlance, a keyword is any word or phrase that a user might type into Google, to find the information they are looking for. "Short-tail" or "head terms" are usually one or two words and are quite general. "Long-tail" keywords are lengthier phrases of at least three or four words.

Here are some examples of short-tail keywords:

- Martial arts
- Karate
- Kickboxing
- MMA

- Self-defence
- Martial arts movies.

You get the idea.

Short-tail keywords are of little use to martial arts school owners. They are incredibly competitive and difficult to rank for, and why the user is interested in the topic (the 'user intent') is often unclear. Someone typing "martial arts" into Google could be looking for movie recommendations or very general information about martial arts. They're not showing any intent to go to a class and don sparring gear.

Long-tail keywords are much more specific and give a clearer idea of what the searcher wants to find. They could also include local modifiers, such as a town or city name. This narrows down their focus further and signals that the user is actively looking for a local club to attend.

Here are some long-tail keyword examples:

- Is karate better than kung fu?
- Full-contact martial arts in New York.
- Taekwondo clubs in South-East London.
- Would Bruce Lee beat Muhammad Ali in a fight?
- Once Upon a Time in China Jet Li.
- Brazilian Jiu-Jitsu classes for adults in Portland.
- Karate classes for children near me.

From reading these examples, you can see the intent behind the search, and Google will have a much better chance of presenting useful, relevant content to the user. As a school owner, target long-tail keywords with a specific geographic focus matching your school's location.

Keywords that end with "near me" will trigger Google's local search algorithm, so you want to ensure you rank for the first part of the keyword, e.g., "**karate clubs** near me". Google will factor in the perceived quality of your website and combine it with your proximity to the searcher. Together, these determine the order in which local karate clubs will appear in the SERPs.

Brand vs non-brand keywords

We can categorise keywords according to whether they are brand-term keywords, or non-brand (generic) keywords. A branded keyword is one that includes your company name or the name of your products. For MA schools, a branded term will revolve around your school's name. You would naturally expect to rank at the top of the results for these keywords within your local area, so you won't need to focus on brand terms too much. You should track your brand terms in your monthly search results monitoring and optimise your site if you do not rank in the first position for your own name.

Customers who already know you and are searching for you by name are likely to find you, regardless. As a result, most of your SEO attention should go towards ranking for generic keywords. Non-brand keywords in the martial arts space will usually involve a combination of the phrase "martial arts", the name of a specific art, a geographic location, or an age group. For example, adults or children. Here are some examples:

- Ju-jitsu classes for adults in Melbourne.
- Kids kung fu lessons near me.

How to perform keyword research

Here is a simple step-by-step process to follow to find the right list of keywords to target. Use your findings to inform your Google Business Profile and website optimisation.

Step 1 - Create a seed list

Brainstorm a list of obvious keywords that you would search for if you were your ideal customer. This will give you a starting point, or 'seed list'. Let's imagine you run a Shotokan karate club in Manchester, UK, and teach children up to adults.

You might brainstorm the following keywords:

- Karate club Manchester
- Karate clubs Manchester
- Manchester karate schools
- Kids Karate Manchester
- Shotokan karate in Manchester
- Manchester martial arts
- Karate for adults in Manchester
- Childrens karate classes in Manchester
- Martial arts for children in Manchester
- Kids martial arts Manchester
- Adults martial arts Manchester.

Now we have our seed list. You could rearrange all the words in many similar combinations, but let's not worry about that for now. Google is clever enough to know that "kids karate Manchester" means the same thing as "karate clubs for children in Manchester". You are likely to end up ranking in a similar position for both, and for other similar phrases.

Step 2 - Google Suggest

Now take your seed list and type each one into Google's search box. Watch the auto-suggest options that are auto-populated beneath the search bar. Here, Google is telling you what other users are searching for using similar words, so write them down and add them to your list.

Google Suggest's autocompleted keyword suggestions

Google Suggest returned the following keyword ideas, based on the seed keywords above:

- Manchester martial arts centre
- Manchester martial arts shop
- Manchester kickboxing
- Manchester karate tournament
- Manchester karate competition
- Toddler karate Manchester
- Manchester adults karate club
- Manchester shotokan karate academy
- Manchester university shotokan karate club.

Take these keywords and discount any that are irrelevant. If you don't teach toddlers, there is little point trying to rank for "toddler karate Manchester". Add the rest to your original list.

Step 3 - Google's related searches

Now enter each of these searches into Google, run the search, and scroll to the bottom of page 1. Here you'll find a list of related searches that Google is helpfully suggesting for you:

Google's related search suggestions

If any of these are relevant, and you don't already have them, guess what? Add them to your list!

Step 4 - Google Keyword Planner

For this step, you need access to Google Keyword Planner. This tool is part of the Google Ads platform, so first you'll need to create a free Google Ads account, if you don't already have one.

Once logged in, ensure your account is in "Expert Mode", then select Tools & Settings > Keyword Planner. Select the "Discover New Keywords" option, and paste your keywords into the box, as shown below. You can enter ten at a time:

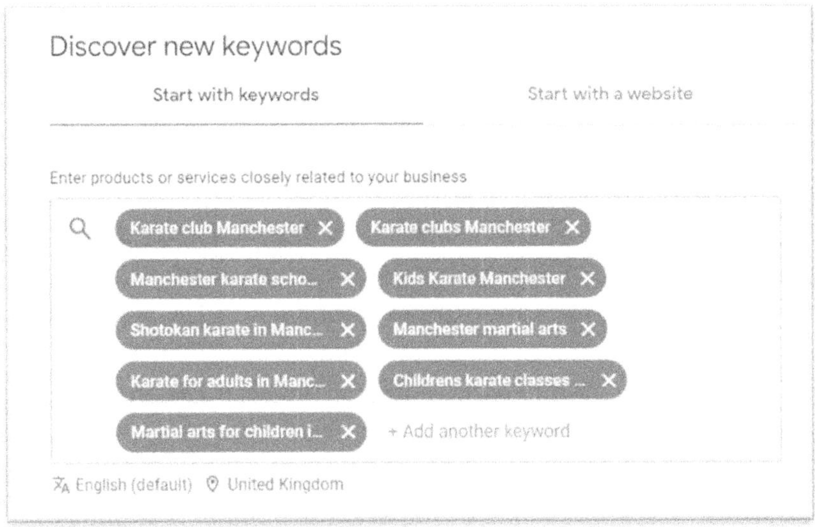

Google Keyword Planner's keyword discovery tool

Then click "Get results".

You will be presented with a list of other suggestions. Most of this list is likely to be other competing martial arts in your area, but if any apply to you, add them to your original list.

Now go back to the main screen for Google Keyword Planner. This time, select "Get Search Volumes & Forecasts":

Google Keyword Planner's search volume tool

On this screen, paste in your list of keywords, or upload them from a spreadsheet if you have recorded them this way, then click "get started". The tool will then look in Google's vast database for all the searches of those keywords in your host country. We're only interested in Manchester, UK, so edit the location at the top of the screen, changing it from "United Kingdom", to "Manchester, England, United Kingdom".

Now you'll see useful, local results for the specific city we care about. Sort your results by the *average number of monthly searches* column. If there are enough searches for a term, Google will show you an estimated range next to the keyword. These are not 100 per cent accurate, and a keyword with zero results may not in fact have had no searches. What we want to find out here is the relative popularity.

The monthly search volume shown matters less than how popular a keyword is, relative to others on the list. The numbers are just broad estimates and should not be taken as fact. Once you have identified the most popular keywords, you can base the rest of your SEO efforts around them. For example, below we can see that "Manchester martial arts" receives significantly more searches per month than "karate club Manchester", even though the numbers shown are a broad range.

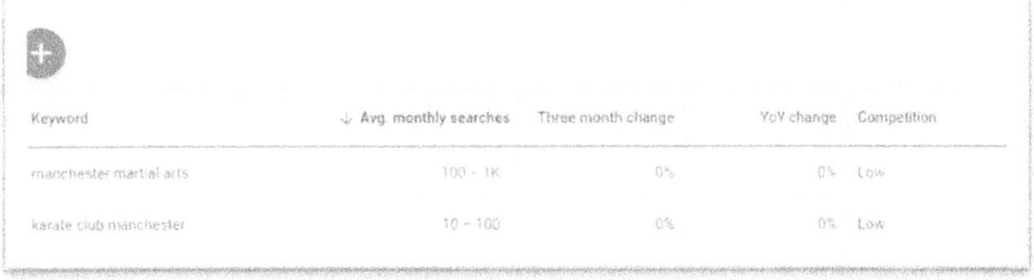

Keyword	↓ Avg. monthly searches	Three month change	YoY change	Competition
manchester martial arts	100 - 1K	0%	0%	Low
karate club manchester	10 – 100	0%	0%	Low

Keyword Planner results screen

You can export the results to a spreadsheet so you can save them for further analysis, or to use for tracking your search positions in the future.

Only five of the twenty keywords have any meaningful search volume. One of them "Manchester martial arts shop" is probably not relevant enough (unless you also run a martial arts shop in Manchester, in which case, target that keyword!).

Of the five, we can also see the "Manchester martial arts" keyword attracts *up to ten times as many searches* as "karate club Manchester". As a karate club owner in Manchester, which of these would you base your website, social media, and Google Business Profile around as a primary keyword? That's right, you would be better off targeting the more generic "martial arts" keywords rather than the style-specific one that might have been your first choice.

It is likely that you will find similar results in your locale. Potential customers usually have a low awareness of specific martial arts. Parents are more interested in finding a quality instructor and a safe, disciplined, positive environment for their child. Nine times out of ten, a club is better off targeting keywords in the following formats:

martial arts [CITY/TOWN NAME]
martial arts in [CITY/TOWN NAME]
[CITY/TOWN NAME] martial arts

For example:

- Edinburgh martial arts
- Martial arts in Doncaster.

For larger metro areas, consider including the borough or district name. For example, "martial arts in Queens, New York".

You can still use your style name as a secondary keyword and include it everywhere appropriate on your website. But the prime keyword, from an SEO perspective, will probably be a variation of "martial arts" plus your location.

Domain names

A perennial question in SEO is to what extent a business's website domain name should contain keywords. Is this likely to increase its ranking for those terms? These days, it is best not to do this unless the keyword makes sense as a part of your school's name. Your domain name is an important part of your brand identity, and should:

- Be short
- Be easy to spell and pronounce
- Have an appropriate top-level domain (TLD) such as .com or .co.uk
- Match your brand name as close as possible.

Google has stated that there is no ranking benefit to including keywords in a domain. Also, try to avoid using hyphens.

Nobody-wants-to-read-or-type-a-domain-like-this.com!

Hyphenated domains are difficult to pronounce if you are telling someone about your website verbally, and annoying to type. Provided your content is strong, your site structure is good, and you adopt the SEO techniques in this book, you should be able to rank for your key terms just as well as anyone else. But if your school's name includes a strong keyword, such as "martial arts" or the name of a specific art, then include it in your domain name.

Action Points

- ☐ Brainstorm a seed keyword list.
- ☐ Expand list using autosuggest and related searches.
- ☐ Expand further using Google Ads Keyword Planner.
- ☐ Add keyword volumes using Keyword Planner.
- ☐ Export your finalised keyword list.

4

HOW TO RANK WITHOUT A WEBSITE

Set up and optimise your Google Business Profile.

Google Business Profile (GBP)[3] is a promotional tool for business owners. It allows detailed business information to appear within search results.

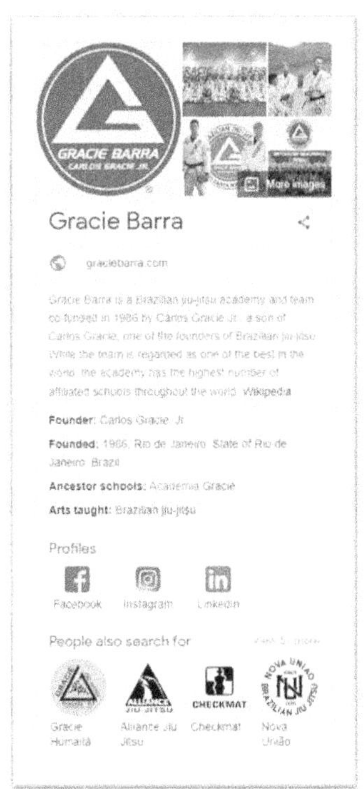

Information from a business's GBP will appear in Google organic results, on Google Maps, and on the Google Knowledge Graph. The Knowledge Graph is the panel of detailed information that sometimes appears along the side of a Google results page (on desktop), or above the normal organic search results (on mobile).

---

[3] Previously known as 'Google My Business' until 2022.

Setting up a GBP is one of the quickest and most effective things a local business can do to improve their local visibility. With GBP you can appear in search even if you do not yet have a website. Setting up and getting a website to rank takes time, but you can register a Google Business Profile, fill it in, and publish it in less than an hour (although verification takes longer).

Why should you have one?

Did you know that 46% of all Google searches have some local intent[4], and that most local searches happen on mobile phones? A local search is said to increase the likelihood of the searcher visiting a shop or business location by 35%. These are big numbers, which prove that every local business needs a local SEO strategy.

Without a GBP, you'll have difficulty controlling the information returned about your school in Google search results. You risk missing out on potential students and leads through lack of visibility in organic search. It will be harder for students to find your website, opening hours, contact details and location. For these reasons, it is important to pay close attention to optimising your business profile for the local search algorithm.

Google Business Profile is free and is easy to set up and maintain. It also integrates with Google Maps, which is one of the primary tools searchers use to find a local business.

---

[4] According to BusinessDIT: https://www.businessdit.com/local-search-statistics

Create your Google Business Profile

To set up your profile, you'll first need to have a Google account, and sign into it. If you have a business-specific email address, it would be sensible to use this to create a Google account and profile, rather than using your personal Gmail. You can create your business profile via Google Maps. Click the menu in the top-left corner of the screen, then select "Add your business" and follow the instructions.

Sometimes, your business will already have a GBP set up, perhaps by an old instructor or team member who has since left, and you do not have access to it. In this case, go to Google Maps, search for your school's name and click on it. Then select "Claim this business" and follow the steps to verify your ownership. Once this is successful, your account will "own" the business and you'll be able to manage and update it as required.

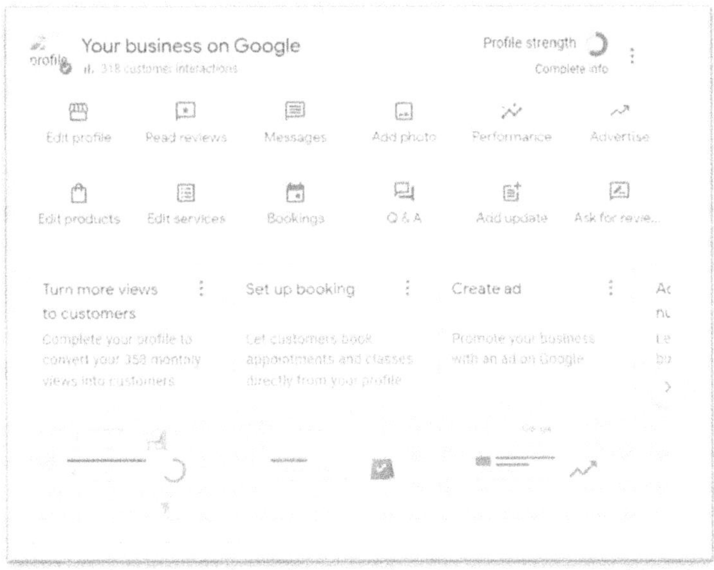

The Google Business Profile admin interface

Verify your profile

Once you have created your profile, it's important to verify it so that you can easily amend your business information in the future. You also want to get verified so that you can drop a pin on your location in Google Maps. Google provides several ways to get verified. The usual method is to ask them to mail a postcard containing a verification code to your address. When you receive the postcard, which could take a week or two, log back into your GBP account and enter the verification code. If you've already verified your website in Google Search Console, this may speed the process up.

Verifying your locations can be difficult if you teach out of hired halls, or leisure or community centres. Often the management of these multi-use facilities won't want your club's name appearing on Google Maps at their address. For leisure centres, you'll likely have to do without a Google Maps But, it can be worth a try to get verified at hired halls. Speak to the hall's management to ask if they will pass on the postcard to you when it arrives. Then you can enter your verification code and your club will get its map pin. You will need to create a separate profile for each location, but you can manage them all in a single account.

I managed to get two of my hired community centres verified so that my club's name displayed in Google Maps, but it took a while, and several attempts. I couldn't verify one venue (a multi-use judo centre), but as the wise Meatloaf once said, "two out of three ain't bad".

Fill out all the GBP fields

Complete as many fields as possible. This will give you the biggest local SEO boost and generate the most meaningful, qualified contacts or web traffic for your school. Work through the setup wizard and fill everything in, including your:

- Business name (this must be accurate and match your legal business or trading name. Don't stuff it with keywords).
- Opening hours.
- Contact details including website address and phone number. Prospects searching on mobile, where most local searches happen, can call you by tapping on your phone number.
- Physical address.
- Business categories.

Choose the right categories

Picking the right primary and secondary categories is vital, so spend some time researching the options. Considering which of Google's pre-defined categories best describes your business. There are several options which apply to martial arts schools, including:

- Martial arts school
- Sports club
- Jiu jitsu school
- Martial arts club
- Self Defence School
- Karate club
- Karate school
- Judo club
- Judo school

- Tae kwon do school
- Kickboxing school
- Kung fu school
- Aikido school
- Boxing gym
- Boxing club.

Among others.

You can include more than one category but try to use as few as possible (up to three or four). Category-stuffing is only likely to confuse Google and make your appearances in search less relevant. For most schools, I recommend putting "Martial arts school" as your primary category, followed by "martial arts club" and a style-specific category as your secondary ones. If you run a full-time, multi-style gym, list your main styles. But don't go overboard and try not to use more than three or four categories in total.

If you're still not sure what categories to pick, research your local competitors. Google won't display the category to users, so to find out, you can download a free Chrome extension called GMB Everywhere. I searched for "martial arts near me", then switched to Google Maps.

This is what I found:

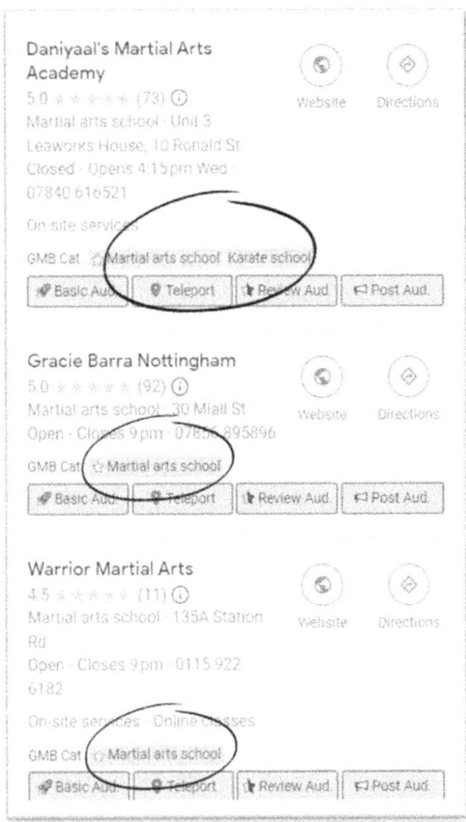

Category research with GMB Everywhere

As you can see, the top three clubs all use "martial arts school" with one to three supporting categories.

Enable messaging

Google Business Profile includes a handy instant messaging feature. To turn it on, search your business name, and the GBP management dashboard will appear within the search results page. Click Messages, then ensure messaging is enabled. You can even set up automated FAQs that customers can pick from. This could save you time and should generate better qualified leads. Frequently asked questions and answers you could set up within the Messaging tool include:

- What age groups do you teach?
- Do I have to be fit/flexible already?
- Do I need previous experience / do you accept beginners?
- What martial arts do you teach?

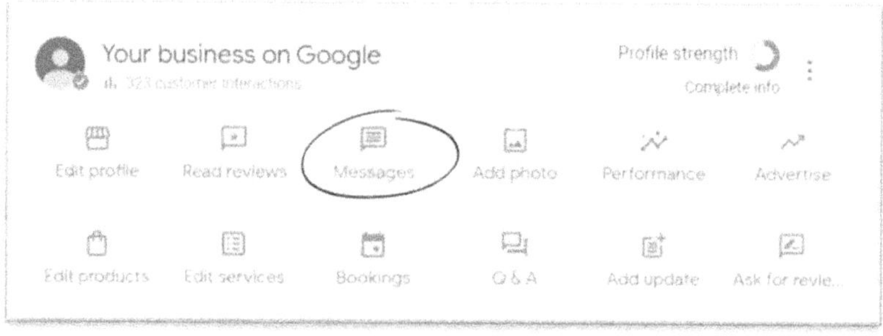

Google Business Profile's messaging settings

Use this feature for general questions, which you've probably already answered on your website, so you can reuse that content here. But don't give out key information such as your prices and timetable. You want potential customers to get in direct contact so that you or your sales team / membership manager or virtual assistant (if you have one) can reach out by telephone. Getting a prospect on the phone is much more likely to lead to a class or induction booking. Exchanging lots of messages back-and-forth can take longer and sometimes results in a lower conversion rate. Your goal should be to hook in the prospect via messaging, then get their phone number and call them to discuss their needs. Speaking to a prospect by phone is the best way to answer their questions efficiently, put them at ease, and get them or their child booked in for a class.

Be sure to enable notifications in your Google Maps app to get instant alerts on your phone of new customer messages. Short response times are much more likely to lead to new students, so don't leave your customers waiting. If you cannot commit to calling all prospects within 24 hours, nominate someone else in your team to own this.

Gain Positive Google Reviews

We'll cover reviews in more depth in chapter five, but one of the most important functions of your Google Business Profile is to showcase real reviews of your business by current or previous students and their parents. So, ensure you have a process for asking for reviews and responding to them swiftly. Getting more, and better, reviews than your local competition will help you stand out as the martial arts centre of excellence in your area and help reduce the cost of acquiring new students in the future.

Post regular updates

Customers and Google want to know that your business is operating and successful, so show them! You can post updates directly through your Google Business Profile, and these display on the search results page. I recommend posting at least once per week, but find a cadence that is sustainable for you. Updates can include interesting news, events, special offers, service updates, opening times, or anything else your audience may find interesting. Include good quality photos with every update, and check your spelling, grammar, and punctuation. This has the secondary benefit of filling up your photo gallery with interesting visual content.

Google provides for three different types of post:

- Updates
- Offers
- Events.

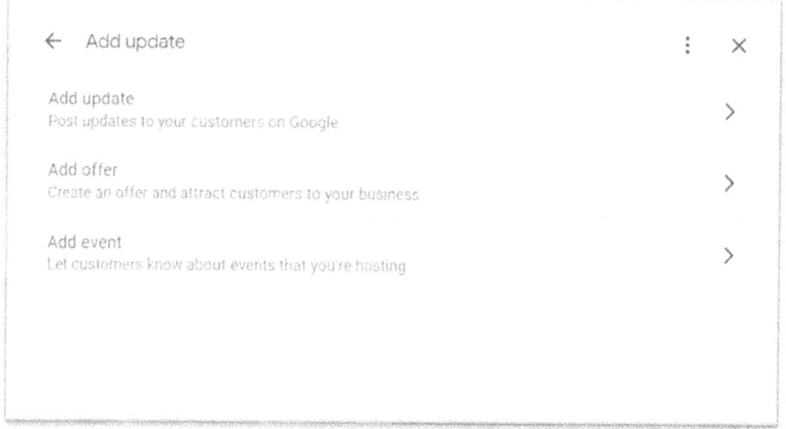

Google Business Profile's add update screen

For general updates, always include a photo and a button which links to a relevant page on your website. The "offer" post type gives you a few extra options, allowing you to set start and end dates for your special offer, as well as a voucher code and any terms and conditions that apply. "Events" can have a specific start time and end time, as well as the start and end date. Think about which post type is most appropriate for each piece of content you share.

Here are a few content ideas for your GBP posts:

- Instructor news and profiles
- Grading announcements and results (with pictures of lots of happy, smiling students)[5]
- Competition results
- Special offers / sign-up packages
- Links to local press coverage of your school
- Opening and closing times, for example during public holidays
- Links to blog posts you've published on your website
- "Behind the scenes" of your gym / school
- Student of the month, star of the week, etc.

In short, your regular GBP posts should be a natural extension of your other organic social media efforts, and you can post the same content. If you get into a regular rhythm of posting to your profile, you should see an improvement in web traffic and leads.

Add UTM tracking to links

GBP posts include a URL field where you can direct traffic to the specific pages on your website. If you'd like to track exactly how many visits or leads you receive from your Google Business Profile, you can add Google's UTM tracking code to the links on your promotional posts. Create UTM code using Google's free Campaign URL Builder[6] tool, setting the

---

[5] Ensure you have consent and a photography/video policy in place.
[6] https://ga-dev-tools.google/campaign-url-builder/

Campaign Source to "GBP" or whatever makes most sense to you.

You can then use Google Analytics to find out how much traffic your website received from your posts. This is nice to have but is not essential. You should only spend time on this if you regularly look at your web analytics and use them to make business decisions. Otherwise, you'll be wasting time you could better spend elsewhere on running your club. To find out more about Google Analytics and how to measure your web traffic, turn to chapter fourteen.

Upload high-quality photos

As we all know, a picture speaks a thousand words. Uploading high-quality and engaging photos to your GBP helps to:

- Show your prospective students your club is popular.
- Give the school a human face, by showing the faces of its humans!
- Demonstrate to Google that you are a real and active business that might be a good fit for what users are searching for.
- Provide insight into your school's culture and what sort of clientele you cater to.

If you operate a full-time academy, show photos of the outside of the building, the car park, the reception, and all your indoor facilities and training areas. If you operate from hired halls, you can still do this, but may want to focus more on your people (students and instructors).

At the time of writing, Google recommends using square images with dimensions of 720px x 720px. If you post images in other sizes, be aware that it may become cropped when displayed on your GBP. Try to use the dimensions above and avoid placing text on the image unless you have first resized it to the correct dimensions. Free tools such as Canva make resizing images for different social platforms incredibly easy.

Pictures of happy staff, students and parents can help to paint a positive picture of what a customer can expect from you. Get permission first from anyone whose face is visible in anything you upload, and/or if you want to mention them by name. You can cover this by using photography and videography, or social media policies, which you can ask students to accept when they set up their memberships.

GBP also allows you to upload video. Here are Google's technical guidelines for photos and videos. Check these yourself in case they have recently changed:

Photo guidelines

Your photos look best on Google if they meet the following standards:

Format: JPG or PNG.

Size: Between 10 KB and 5 MB.

Recommended resolution: 720 px tall, 720 px wide.

Minimum resolution: 250 px tall, 250 px wide.

Quality: The photo should be in focus, well-lit, and have no significant alterations or excessive use of filters. The image should represent reality.

Video guidelines

Make sure your videos meet the following requirements:

Duration: Up to 30 seconds long

File size: Up to 75 MB

Resolution: 720p or higher

Showcase your services

Your GBP is an opportunity to showcase your brand and the products and services you provide, so treat it like a virtual shop window. It includes an area for listing your services and another space for uploading product details. Fill these in carefully to showcase what you do. Services are listed in simple text fields, but the products section allows you to include a photo, title, description, price, product category, and even a call-to-action button. This allows prospective customers to view and make purchase decisions without ever hitting your website.

For martial arts schools, I would suggest avoiding the product listing feature. Even if you sell branded merch, you probably won't want to come across as too commercial, and your customers are your students, not the public. But you should list your services using the text fields provided and associate them with the relevant categories you set earlier.

For example, your listing might look something like this:

Martial Arts School [category]

- Kickboxing classes
- Adult kickboxing
- Junior kickboxing
- Teen kickboxing
- Sport karate
- MMA
- Private tuition.

Self Defence School [category]

- Corporate self-defence courses
- Community self-defence classes
- Private self-defence classes.

List all your services, but only include those that your school offers. Hoping to attract more visitors, it can be tempting to list all the remotely related services you can, but remember that users can suggest edits to your profile. If you promote services that are not actually offered by your school, one of your competitors may flag this with Google. Revisit the list when things change to keep it up to date.

Include your key search terms

Include the keywords your customers use to find you in your profile and posts. Most potential students, and especially their parents, don't appreciate the differences between martial arts. Most of the time, they'll be using the keyword "martial arts" when searching, unless they have a greater understanding and a specific art in mind. Or they might search for "karate" because that's what they have heard of.

As a school owner, I know that nobody searches for my specific art, as it is not a household name. Whilst I tracked my local search rankings by style name, most of my efforts went into optimising my Google Business Profile, website and social media for keywords relating to "martial arts", because that is where the search volume is. Incorporate your chosen keywords and town name into your GBP description.

A word of warning here –don't stuff keywords into your business name field. Other users can suggest edits to your profile to Google. While you may get some benefits from adding keywords to your profile's business name, it's likely that one of your competitors will flag the inconsistency with Google and they will change your name back to match your website or legal entity.

Action Points

- ☐ Create and verify your Google Business Profile.
- ☐ Fill in as many fields as possible.
- ☐ Determine the best categories and add them.
- ☐ Switch on the messaging function.
- ☐ Post updates at least once per week.
- ☐ Upload high-quality images and videos.
- ☐ Ask students and parents for reviews.
- ☐ Create a process for requesting reviews.

5

THE FEEDBACK LOOP

The importance of customer reviews.

Google reviews are an oft overlooked but crucial aspect of local SEO. The star ratings you'll see below your business name in the Knowledge Graph (the panel in the search results that displays your company info), serve a double purpose.

We all know that social proof is a powerful thing, and most users pay attention to reviews when shopping online. Of these, more than half will travel further, or spend more, on a brand that has a better reputation than the competition. Customers are much more likely to believe honest feedback from other customers than to take your fantastic conversion-focussed marketing copy at face value.

So, ensure above all that you're providing excellent service to your customers. Once you've nailed this, you are creating the right conditions to receive positive reviews.

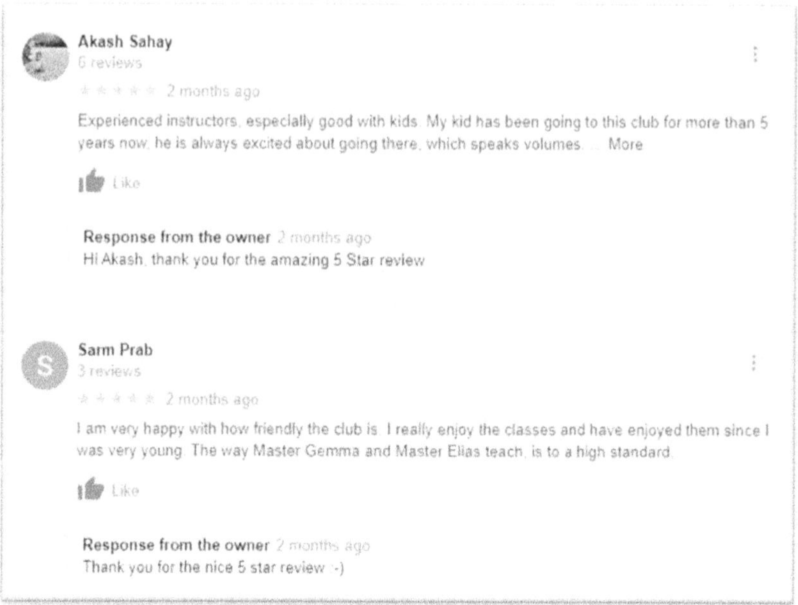

Examples of Google reviews

Google's local search algorithm includes customer reviews as a ranking factor. They play a direct and important role in your business's prominence in local search. The number and quality of reviews will affect how high you appear in search, and whether you show up in the all-important "Local Pack" or "3-Pack". This is the panel of three featured sites that sometimes appears above the normal organic results. Because Google values word-of-mouth, it knows that businesses which attract positive user sentiment are offering quality products or services.

Look at these statistics from local search software provider SOCi[7]:

- Conversion of Google profiles improves by 44% when a business increases its average rating by one full star.
- For every 10 new reviews earned, conversion of Google profiles improves by 2.8%.
- For every 25% of reviews responded to, conversion of Google profiles improves by 4.1%.

So, it's time to take Google reviews seriously and to build a simple process for obtaining and responding to them.

Look at this search for martial arts schools in Birmingham:

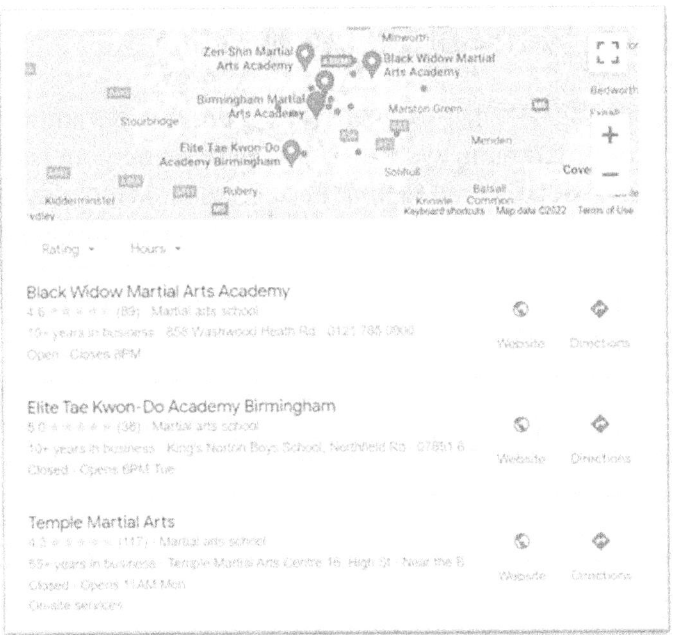

Local Pack results for Birmingham, UK

---

[7] https://www.meetsoci.com/resources/insights/brands-franchises/state-of-google-reviews-research-report-syn

What do they all have in common? That's right - lots of positive reviews.

But how do you get reviews, I hear you cry? Simple – ask your customers! Either ask them in person or set up an email automation that fires out to students and asks them to leave you a positive review. From the GBP dashboard you can generate a link which you can embed in your emails. It will take your customer straight to a screen where they can type their review, for a seamless and hassle-free experience. Click "Ask for review" on the dashboard to find the link. The only downside is that users need to have a Google account, so will need to sign in or create one.

Automate the process

I recommend setting up an automated email programme via your email marketing system or school management software. Many MA-specific management software tools include some level of automation, although it may be basic. Compare this with what your email tool can do, if you use a separate email marketing system as well. For example, MailChimp and Mailerlite both include powerful automation features that will allow you to trigger specific email campaigns based on criteria you choose. You can set emails to fire out to individuals based on when they joined the list, when they became a student, on their birthday, or many other triggers.

At my school, I used MailChimp to send emails to my students approximately three months after they joined my school. The only manual step was to "tag" each contact as a student. I used two tags, one for juniors (i.e., their parents), and one for adults. Doing this allows you to tailor the language in your triggered email for each group. I then created an email campaign which contained Google's "leave a review" link to my Google Business Profile's review page. This prevents the student from having to think about what to do and how to do it, and makes the process as simple as possible. All they must do is click the link, spend a few moments writing a review, and decide on a star rating.

Next, think about when to email. Send it too soon, in the days or weeks after they joined, and the student won't feel they have enough to go on. Leave it too late, bearing in mind the high drop-out rate in martial arts, and you'll miss out on review opportunities. Experiment and see what works best for you.

Think about other methods and times you can ask for reviews. Your students may not see that one email, so you may like to ask them twice, but space out the requests. You could even put a poster up in your reception area or have printed cards on the reception desk. If your club has a band of dedicated students and loyal followers, or even entire families who train with you, these people are likely to leave you a glowing review, if asked. Ask your instructors to mention it at the end of class. If you have just delivered a fantastic, high energy, exciting class and everyone finished pumped and enthused, capitalise on this by asking for a review, and tell them how they can leave one.

Make the process as effortless as possible. Get creative about how and when you ask for reviews, and you'll receive a steady stream of them, which is what Google wants to see.

As with most other aspects of search, keywords play an important role in customer reviews too. If you have a series of recent reviews which mention the services you want to appear for, your "score" in the Google algorithm will get a boost. When asking for reviews, you may want to suggest to your students that they include certain keywords, for example "Martial arts in [your town or city]" or "kids [specific MA style] in [town or city]".

Be responsive

Aim to post a reply to all reviews within 24 hours, as your responsiveness also signals to Google about the quality of your customer service. Even if you get a negative review, respond swiftly, helpfully, and fairly. How a business handles negative reviews speaks volumes about their culture and professionalism, so don't ignore them. People understand you cannot please everyone, so use the situation to your advantage, or at least limit the damage. Customers prefer responsive businesses, as does Google.

Appeal spurious negative reviews

Sometimes, a business may receive negative reviews through no fault of their own. Sometimes this can happen because of nefarious tactics by a competitor, where they leave fake reviews. Google has a process for requesting review takedowns, which may be worth a try, but success is not guaranteed. To report a review, open Google Maps and find your school, then expand the reviews. Click the three dots next to the review and select "report review". You'll then see a list of reasons why you want to report the review. Select the most appropriate one and submit.

Alternatively, if you have a genuinely disgruntled customer, reach out to them and try to resolve their issue. If you can turn the situation around and resolve their problem, they may amend or remove their original review.

When reviews are first posted, Google checks them against its prohibited and restricted content policy[8]. It does this to filter out spammy, fake reviews and those with offensive content. But Google won't know who your real customers are. Ultimately, the best way to deal with negative reviews is to drown them out with lots of positive ones. People are used to seeing the occasional negative review and may even be suspicious of businesses with a perfect five-star score. So don't stress too much if you get an occasional whingebag popping up in your Google Business Profile reviews. Instead, double-down on encouraging new, positive reviews to drown out the dissenters.

Facebook reviews

Facebook Pages also allow for customer reviews. It's useful to gain as many of these as possible, particularly if you use your Facebook page, or Facebook ads, as a key part of your marketing strategy.

Facebook reviews do not contribute to your Google rankings, so it is better to ask your students and parents to leave reviews on Google instead. Yet, this doesn't mean that you should ignore Facebook's reviews. As one of the largest social networks, Facebook is a big search engine in its own right and a valuable source of traffic to your website. Your Facebook page may even rank on the first page of Google for brand-name searches, so you want it to be as enticing as possible to new prospects.

---

[8] https://support.google.com/local-guides/answer/7400114?hl=en-GB

In summary, Google reviews are vital for your local search visibility. Facebook reviews are not essential, but try to attract some anyway if you can - but not at the expense of your Google reviews.

Action Points

- ☐ Create a review request email template.
- ☐ Automate the sending process.
- ☐ Respond to all reviews within 24 hours.
- ☐ Appeal fake reviews.

6

ON-PAGE SEO FUNDAMENTALS

Learn how to improve your pages and get them ranking.

This chapter will delve into the tried-and-tested techniques of on-page SEO. Like a front kick or a right cross, these basics have stood the test of time and are a great foundation on which to build. As you will never be able to perform a flying side kick without first learning the standing version, so your website will never reach the heights of Google SERPs if these foundational elements of SEO are absent.

On-page SEO includes these key elements:

- Metadata
- Headings
- Page content
- Page structure and layout
- Internal linking
- Image optimisation
- Descriptive URLs
- Technical SEO.

Technical SEO requires more advanced knowledge and tools, so we'll look at that later in the book.

On-page, or on-site search engine optimisation is the term used to describe the many techniques and tactics that a website owner has direct control over. They are things you can change on your website to get it to rank higher in search.

It is important to get this right before spending too much time and energy on off-site SEO (backlink building) as it is harder and more time consuming. Your web pages are within your own control (or should be) and are easy to update.

Basic SEO isn't rocket surgery. Most martial arts club websites are old, have a poor user experience and minimal optimisation. So, it doesn't take much for you to leapfrog your competitors in the rankings, even if they are much longer established schools. Sometimes, large professionally run schools have bigger marketing budgets and may contract out their web development to an agency. They can be harder to beat given the amount of traffic and backlinks they receive, but even super-slick sites often have poor SEO.

When conducting SEO, think about setting realistic expectations. In the towns I taught in, there were large, full-time, multi-style martial arts gyms which each had hundreds of students. My classes ran on a part-time basis out of hired halls. I knew I was unlikely to beat these large schools in the short term for generic "martial arts" keywords. Instead, I set my sights on ranking right below these schools for the generic terms, and on trying to beat them for my style-specific keywords.

What are the goals of on-page SEO?

You want to optimise your website to:

- Show Google that your page is the best, most relevant fit for a user's search intent, for the page's target keywords.
- Give users the information they want and expect.
- Engage the user, so they spend longer on your site and explore other pages or get in convert into a lead.
- Reduce your bounce rate (the proportion of single-page visits where a user takes no action and leaves).

Metadata

Metadata is a term used to describe information that describes a web page, rather than the contents of the page that the user reads. Metadata is held in meta tags, which are lines of HTML code within each page, which tell search engines or web browsers important information about the page.

The two main meta tags that you need to concern yourself with are:

- Meta title
- Meta description.

Meta title

Web browsers use the meta title to know what to display on the browser tab, at the very top of the screen:

BBC News meta title

In this example, “Home - BBC News” is the title tag for the BBC News home page. Google also displays the tag’s contents in the SERPs, and it appears on social media posts when someone shares the page. In Google search results, it is the large blue clickable title below the domain name.

Here are some examples:

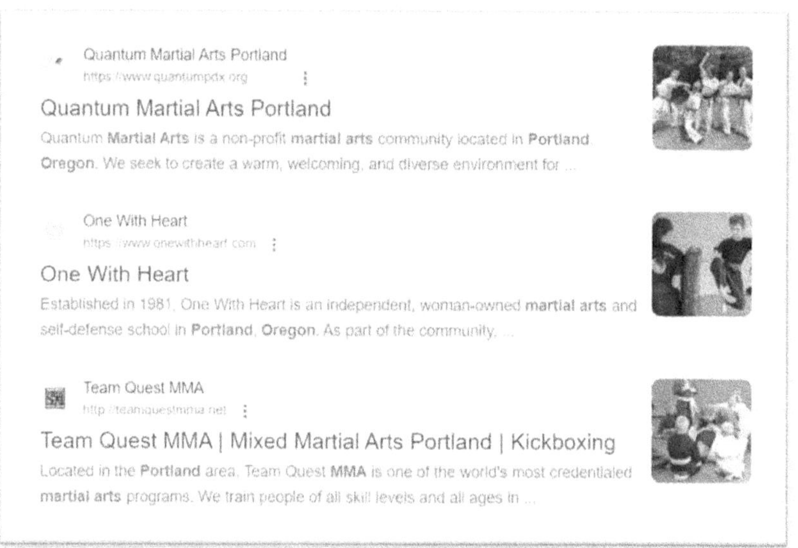

Meta titles shown in SERPs

The large title immediately below the domain name comes from the meta title tag, in most cases. Sometimes Google's algorithm decides it can come up with a more descriptive title itself and will replace the title you have defined on your page. There is no way to completely avoid this, or to get it changed back if it happens to your site. But we can do our best to avoid this happening by being clear and descriptive with our title tags and keeping them to an appropriate length. Meta titles are one of the single most important factors for on-page SEO, so take your time and get them right.

Tag length

The ideal length of a meta title is 50-60 characters. Anything longer and Google may truncate it, resulting in keywords being cut off the end when displayed. If this happens, it will lose a bit of its impact with users and your click through rate may suffer. You can replace words with symbols (e.g., replacing 'and' with '&') to save on space.

Avoid duplication

Never use the same meta title for more than one page. Each should be unique, otherwise Google may struggle to understand the unique purpose of each page.

Include your keywords

Each page on your site should have a primary keyword that you want it to target. Include this keyword in the title tag, at or near the beginning. Keywords at the start of a meta title have more SEO weight than those at the end.

Consider the example of a page about karate classes for children. The title tag may look like this:

Children's Karate Classes | Fulham, London | ABC Martial Arts

In this example, the key search term that a parent might use is "children's karate classes", so this goes at the front. We also include a location, as the parent may search for "children's karate classes in London" or "children's karate classes near me". Last, we include the school's name, as it is less likely to be part of a search term but is still important brand information. A vertical pipe separates each term, so that it is clear to users and search engines that these are distinct but related pieces of information. The whole tag is 52 characters long - well within the guidelines.

If we wanted to get even more specific and use the full 60-character limit, we could instead use:

Childrens Karate Classes | Fulham, London | ABC Martial Arts

Don't obsess about going over the character limit, particularly if your business name is on the longer side. It won't harm your rankings, but Google may truncate it in search results. If your title tag is going over 60 characters, consider removing your brand name to free up space for more important information. Also avoid writing your title tags in CAPITALS, as they take up more space, and increase the likelihood of Google truncating or replacing your title.

Action Points

- ☐ Add a meta title to each page.
- ☐ Check that all titles are unique.
- ☐ Include your primary keyword for the page.
- ☐ Include location keywords.
- ☐ Keep all titles to 60 characters or fewer.

Meta description

The meta description is a brief passage of text which summarises what a page is about. They do not directly affect your page's position in the search results, but are still very important. A well-written meta description will:

1. Help your page (and brand) stand out among the competition in the search results.
2. Show how your page is relevant to the searcher's intent and entice them in.
3. Increase the click-through-rate (CTR) from SERPs to your website.

There is no maximum character count for a meta description, but in practice Google cuts them off after about 160 characters, so you should aim for up to 155. This is a range rather than an exact number, as Google measures the amount of space needed to display them in pixel width, not by the number of characters. Given that different letters have varying widths, it is difficult to predict exactly where a sentence will be cut off.

An effective description will describe what the page is about and will include the primary keyword you want the page to rank for. If space allows, finish it with a call to action and tell the user what you want them to do, such as "read more", "learn more" or "discover more".

Adrenaline MMA
https://www.adrenalinemma.ca

Adrenaline MMA Training & Fitness Center | London, ON

Adrenaline is a professional **MMA** and athletic training facility that specializes in enhancing all levels of athletic performance and personal fitness.

Classes · Schedule · Instructors · About

Example meta description displayed in Google results

In the above example, returned for a search on "MMA London Ontario", we can see that the keywords "MMA", "training" and "fitness" are all present in both the meta title and description. The end of the sentence is not cut off, and it is clear what the website is about before I click on it.

Descriptions (and titles) should be unique, so it is worth checking that you don't have any duplicate metadata on your site. SEO audit tools can help automate this and save you time. They should match the content of the target page - the description should be accurate and set the user's expectation of what they will find when they arrive on the page. Otherwise, you may find your bounce rate going up as users click straight back to the SERPs. A high bounce rate (or low engagement rate) can harm your rankings.

Within WordPress websites, you can add both the meta title and meta description to pages using any of several SEO plugins.

The most popular SEO plugins for WordPress are:

- Yoast
- RankMath
- All In One SEO Pack.

Yoast, for example, generates page titles and descriptions for you, but it is always best to write your own, so you can optimise them carefully.

If you're using a different content management system for your website, for example Squarespace or Wix, these settings will be in a different place. Squarespace has them under the "SEO" tab for each page.

Action Points

- ☐ Add a meta description to each page on your site.
- ☐ Make each one unique.
- ☐ Limit them to 155 characters at most.
- ☐ Include your primary keyword for the page.
- ☐ Include a call to action if space allows.
- ☐ Check your meta descriptions every few months.

Headings

The intelligent use of headings and sub-headings matters in on-page SEO. Headings tell the user and search engines what a page is about. They identify the major topics and sub-topics of the page. Whereas meta titles only show up in search results and the top of browser tabs, headings do display on the page.

In the code, headings are defined using up to six pairs of HTML tags. For example:

<h1>This is a Heading 1</h1>

<h2>This is a Heading 2</h2>

There is ongoing debate in the SEO world over (amongst many other things) how important heading tags are, and how many are necessary. Conventional SEO wisdom says that every page should have a single H1, for the main page header. Usually this is the first and largest heading on the page, within the top banner area, or the main heading on a blog post.

H2-H6 headings are used to divide up body text, and you may use as many as you need to of each type, provided the page is logical and easy to read. I usually only use H2 and H3, and rarely use H4-H6, as going that far down a hierarchy often means the page is becoming too complicated. Users want short, defined chunks of text they can skim-read, as people rarely read web pages linearly. The eyes dart around to different sections and headings, rather than reading everything left-to-right.

For a martial arts programme landing page, you would divide each key chunk of information and give it a descriptive heading. The heading should contain the keywords for which you want the page to rank.

Let's use an example of a ladies' kickbox fitness class. Rather than showing a big impenetrable wall of text on the page, you might divide the page into the following sections:

What is Ladies Kickbox Fitness?

Get fitter, faster

Lose weight the fun way

Empower yourself through cardio fitness kickboxing

Timetable

Fees

Location

How to book

There are many other ways to structure this page, and you may prefer using different language. But each section, whether it covers the benefits of the class, or more specific features and details, should have its own heading. I would use heading 2 for each of these main sections, then if you need to go into more detail within a section, add a heading 3. For example, under Location, an H2, I may want to add "How to find us" or "directions" as an H3.

Using this HTML markup helps both users and search engines to understand your page. Most content management systems will have a drop list within the front-end page editor, allowing you to choose which heading type you want to use. SEO audit tools such as Screaming Frog can help you identify pages with missing or duplicate H1s.

Action Points

- ☐ Check every page has a single, unique H1 heading.
- ☐ Use smaller headings in a logical structure.
- ☐ Include keywords in your headings.

Page Content

When we talk about content, we mean the words on the page, as well as images and video, downloadable resources, or interactive tools your site may have.

In SEO, content is king! The quality of information you present on your website is the single most important factor for ranking at the top of the search results. Google wants to present the highest quality, most comprehensive and relevant pieces of content to its users. It wants to return the best matches for the terms users are searching on. For this to happen, you need to craft interesting pages which exactly match the intent of your target audience. Besides, one of the other most important ranking factors is the number and quality of backlinks your pages attract. Guess what? Nobody wants to link to poor content.

When writing your web pages, try to make them comprehensive, but without padding them out or waffling. Always check content for spelling and grammar, as any mistakes here scream that you lack attention to detail. This can make even a great business look unprofessional. Web content, particularly for sales or lead-generation pages, should be in the second person rather than the third person. Using the words "you will" rather than "students will" creates a direct connection with the reader and makes it much easier to communicate the benefits of your classes.

Consider the following two examples:

"At our self-defence classes, participants learn a variety of simple techniques to defend themselves against an attack and keep themselves safe at all times. They learn how to recognise the danger signs and de-escalate conflict before it goes too far."

Or:

"At our self-defence classes, you will learn a variety of simple techniques to keep yourself safe from attack. You'll learn how to spot the danger signs and use verbal de-escalation to avoid dangerous situations."

Which paragraph felt more immediate and compelling to you? I'm guessing the second one. Speaking directly to your reader, using the active voice, is much more persuasive than writing in the third person.

Focus keywords

As we discussed earlier in the book, every page should have a primary keyword that you want it to rank for. The goal is to get a page to rank as high as possible for as many relevant terms as you can, to drive ever more traffic. Within the Yoast SEO plugin for WordPress, there is a field called "focus keyword" where you can enter the term you are targeting. Yoast will then assess how well optimised your page content is for the keyword. Other plugins work in a similar way. If your web CMS lacks this feature, write the primary keyword for each page down somewhere for reference. If you are using Yoast, take its optimisation score with a pinch of salt. Don't become obsessed with making the score go green (it uses a traffic light system) on every page, but use it as a general guide.

To stand the best chance of ranking for your keyword, use it several times within the page, including in the H1 header, and within the body text. The primary keyword should appear in the first paragraph, and anywhere else on the page that it makes sense to include it. Use variations of your primary keyword elsewhere in the page, and in subheadings.

Let's take the example of a page called "Adult Taekwondo" - the main landing page for the adults' programme at our fictional club. The primary keyword (based on our earlier keyword research) is also "adult taekwondo". To rank for this in your local area, you could take the following approach:

- Use a Heading 1 of "Adult Taekwondo".
- Use the phrase again within the first paragraph (and in your metadata).

- Use a variety of H2 and/or H3 subheadings, which may include:
    - Why should adults learn taekwondo?
    - What are taekwondo classes like for adults?
    - Adult taekwondo class times / Adult taekwondo timetable.
    - Contact us to book a free adult taekwondo class.
- Add a few FAQs near the bottom of the page, answering some other common questions.
- Pepper the page text with similar keyword variations, e.g., “taekwondo for adults”, “40+ taekwondo”, “adult martial arts classes” etc.

Over time, Google’s AI algorithm is becoming ever more intelligent and can understand how similar phrases relate to the same concept. It is unnecessary (and unwise) to shoehorn the same keyword into your content as many times as possible. This sort of thing worked a few years ago, but now is likely to annoy your readers and harm your rankings. Your page should not look like it was written for search engines, but for real people. Write in a fluid, easy-to-read style and weave your keywords into the text in a natural and organic manner. Break content up into digestible chunks of a few paragraphs each, with descriptive sub-headings. This structure is easy for a busy reader to skim and helps Google to understand what your page is about.

Content length

How long should your content be? The answer, as usual in SEO, is “it depends”. There is no "correct" length for a page, and it very much depends on what type of page you are looking at, and what function it serves. A "contact us" page is short by necessity, as the overriding concern is to give the reader your contact details and/or encourage them to fill in a form. SEO is secondary here.

Search engines currently favour longer content, not because it is long, but because it is naturally more comprehensive, and so the perceived quality is higher. Search engines may regard any page shorter than about 300 words as "thin content" and it will be unlikely to rank well. As a rule of thumb, I recommend aiming for one thousand words for a main landing page or a blog post. Sometimes a blog post may be closer to 1,500 words or more, to do a topic justice. We'll take a closer look at content marketing and blogs later in the book.

Action Points

- ☐ Always check spelling and grammar.
- ☐ Be clear and concise.
- ☐ Optimise content for the page's primary keyword.
- ☐ Avoid thin content.

Page structure and layout

We've looked at headings and sub-headings and discussed how to write content for the biggest impact. But what other things should you consider when building a web page?

White space

White space is your and your reader's friend. When people read a web page, they rarely read left-to-right along each line, as they would when reading the page of a book. Instead, the eye jumps around all over the page. Many years ago, internet usability experts identified the 'F-shaped reading pattern'. Researchers realised during eye-tracking studies that readers scan the first couple of lines, then look down the left edge of the page as they search for key information. The eye alights on key phrases at the start of paragraphs or on sub-headings, but most words on the page are not read.

Clear subheadings containing keywords are so important, as they will catch the eye and draw the reader into looking closer at that section of text. White space makes it easier for the eye to skip around on the page. It allows blocks of content to 'breathe' and requires less concentration by the reader. Blank space does not have to be white, depending on your web design, but usually is.

It is also important to avoid excessively long sentences or ones that span the full width of the screen. They are tiring to read, hence why many sites use generous padding on each side and restrict the content to a central column. This is another example of the use of white space.

Get visual

We can also separate content out using engaging, relevant images or embedded video. After all, a picture speaks a thousand words. Video is even better, but be careful that it does not have a negative impact on your page loading speed.

Unless you're starting out and you have no photos or video of your school and students in action, try to avoid using stock photography. You will always make a better impression on users, and Google, if you use original visual assets you have created yourself.

If you use your own photos and video, they must be of high quality and look professional. Poor image quality can make your club look amateur compared to the slick operation on the other side of town that invested in a professional photo shoot. If you are just starting out, you don't need to go to those lengths yet, but use photos which are well lit, clear and sharp. I was lucky enough to find a professional photographer who specialised in sports and wanted to expand his portfolio. He photographed my students on two occasions during a normal class. The results were stunning, and best of all, free! Ask your students, friends, or family - the chances are that you will know at least one amateur photographer who owns professional-grade cameras and knows how to use them.

Clear calls-to-action (CTAs)

Calls-to-action (CTAs) are how you ask your users to do a specific thing on your site. They are usually links or buttons. Most of the time for an MA school, your CTA will be to get in contact via phone/email or fill in a lead form, as you should optimise all your pages to generate leads. CTAs can take the form of in-text links, buttons, or embedded forms. Use clear, action-oriented wording in your CTAs, such as:

- Get in touch now
- Contact us
- Claim your free trial

- Book your intro session
- Download brochure.

You should use CTAs liberally on your key conversion-focussed landing pages. These are likely to be your home page, programme pages, or location pages, depending on how you have structured your website. For other informational content, such as your blog posts, consider including a single CTA at the end of the post.

For example, a programme page for your Little Ninjas age 4-6 programme might have:

- A contact form embedded on the page after all the key programme information.
- A button 'above the fold' (visible when the page loads without scrolling) which links down to the contact form.

Avoid using 'click here' text in calls to action). This gives no clue to the user about what will happen when they click, and lacks context, making it harder for Google to understand.

A blog post may only have a single CTA button at the end of the post, or an in-text hyperlink to your contact or booking page.

Action Points

- ☐ Use white space to break up your content.
- ☐ Use images and video (where appropriate).
- ☐ Include clear calls-to-action.

Internal linking

Internal links are hyperlinks between pages on a website. External links are those between different websites or domains. They can take several forms:

- Header navigation menus
- Footer links
- In-text (contextual) links
- Sidebar links (e.g., in blog posts)
- Buttons (calls to action)
- Image links.

Internal links are important for SEO because they:

- Improve user experience, allowing visitors to spend more time on your site and consume more content. This improves your site engagement and lowers your bounce rate.
- Provide routes for search engine spiders to find and index your pages.
- Pass link authority or 'link juice' between pages
- Create logical connections between related information on a website, improving topical authority.

User experience

Visitors to your site must be able to navigate around with ease. Your site's main navigation bar is the main way users can find what they want, but site menus are often complicated and confusing. This is often a particular issue for large sites. It is good practice to provide in-text hyperlinks as well between related pages, bearing in mind the ideal journey you would like your user to take. From the home page, provide clear links to your individual programme pages, as well as to your web lead form.

Homepage links could include:

- Tiny Tots
- Young Masters
- Cadets
- Adult Martial Arts.

And / or have a page for each style if you offer more than one art:

- Judo
- Brazilian Jiu-Jitsu
- Kickboxing
- MMA.

Likewise, each age group programme page should link to the style page(s) they apply to, and vice versa.

Example website main navigation menu

Search engine spidering

Internal links improve the ease of navigation for human users. But they also provide a vital route for search engine bots to crawl your site and identify all the pages. Bots will click through your internal links and analyse the pages they find, as well as how they relate to each other. Internal linking prevents bots having to rely solely on your XML sitemap and helps search engines to index and understand your site structure.

Check your site every now and again for 'orphan' pages (pages with no internal links to them), as they may not have been indexed. Orphan pages sometimes arise when information becomes out of date, such as events, seminars, and gradings that have happened in the past. If this content is out of date, remove it rather than leaving it orphaned. If it is still relevant, add at least one link to it from another page.

Dedicated SEO audit tools can identify orphaned pages, but for a quick look at what pages Google includes in its index, use Google's site operator.

On Google, type into the search by **site:** then your domain name, e.g.

site:mymartialartsschool.com

This will return a list of all pages that Google knows about and includes in search results. Scan down the list and check all your key pages appear. Then compare the number of search results with the number of pages in your content management system or listed in your Google Analytics reports. If the Google search results show many fewer pages than your site actually has, this may indicate that some are not being crawled.

Link authority

Link authority, or 'link juice', is the relative importance that Google ascribes to a page. Let's say you have a high authority page on your website that Google thinks is an appropriate result for a specific search term, e.g., "BJJ in Birmingham". By providing internal links to other relevant pages, Google transfers some of the authority from the first page to the second.

Let's say you've written a blog post that ranks very high on a specific subject. By linking it to your most relevant programme page, Google transfers some of the original authority, and the target page may rank higher for similar terms. By cross-linking relevant pages to each other, not only are you helping users find the right information, but you are also maximising the ranking potential of those pages.

Internal linking good practice

If you have a lot of useful blog posts, linking them to each other will create content clusters with topical authority. Your site's overall rankings may improve as a result. Link blog posts to your conversion-focussed programme pages, where relevant. Your primary goal for your martial arts school website should be to generate leads and enquiries, so bear this in mind when deciding what pages to link to.

Think about how to funnel site traffic towards your programme pages. You should have crafted these pages to generate as many bookings or form submissions as possible. You may miss some of these opportunities if visitors instead click away to an instructor page detailing how many championships you've won or how many belts you have. This may help your ego but will not grow your business (newsflash - nobody cares!).

Make it obvious where your internal links are going, so the user doesn't have to guess about what they will find if they click. Avoid cryptic link text such as "click here", "learn more", or single-word links. Instead, use descriptive words to make it clear what users will find. You don't need have to match the focus keyword of the target page exactly, but if you can include a keyword, that's great.

Look at the following examples for a link to a Ladies Kickboxing page with the target keyword "ladies kickboxing in Toronto", from the home page:

GOOD:

Want to get fitter and learn valuable self-defence skills in a safe and supporting environment? Check out our kickboxing classes for ladies.

BAD:

Want to get fitter and learn valuable self-defence skills in a safe and supporting environment? Click here to find out more.

The link in the first example is specific, descriptive and provides clarity to users and to Google of what the target page is about. It uses similar language to the primary keyword for that page. The second example gives no context at all.

Don't go crazy with the internal linking. Try to include at least two internal links on each page, but no more than five or six, unless it is a particularly long page. Overdoing the internal links looks spammy and unnatural to search engines and makes content harder to read if there are links in every sentence or paragraph.

You want to funnel your website visitors towards your 'money pages', which in this case are your programme pages containing your lead form, so it's a great idea to link to a programme page from every blog post. This will make it easy for your visitors to find out what classes are available and how to enquire. It will also pass some 'link juice' from each blog post to your target programme page. Over time, this should push your programme pages higher up search results, which is what we want.

Action Points

- ☐ Use internal links to connect related pages.
- ☐ Use brief, descriptive link text to provide context.
- ☐ Avoid generic link text such as "click here".
- ☐ Incorporate keywords in link text.
- ☐ Link blog posts to programme pages.
- ☐ Link other secondary pages to programme pages.

Image Optimisation

Given that so much SEO revolves around keywords and content, you could be forgiven for thinking that the text on a page is all that matters. However, optimising your images is an important aspect of SEO. Images enrich a page for users, but search engines cannot see and understand them as a human would, so we have some work to do to provide information about the pictures we use.

ALT text

ALT text is a short phrase added to an image which describes it and provides context. Providing descriptive ALT text helps Google to understand what an image is about and how it relates to the text. Ideally, it should include one of the page's target keywords. Good ALT text also increases the chance of your images appearing in Google Image Search.

ALT text is an HTML attribute of the IMG tag, which is the piece of code on a web page that tells the browser to display a specific image. In HTML markup, it looks like this:

<img src="boy-high-kicking.jpg" alt="A boy performing a side kick" />

Content management systems all have a field for ALT text which you can fill in when you upload an image to a page or to your CMS' image library. In WordPress, you upload images to the Media Centre, and you can view the ALT tag for an image by clicking on it from here. As well as providing an SEO benefit, ALT text is crucial to accessibility. Screen-reading software for visually impaired website users reads the ALT text on an image out loud. This helps users to understand what's happening on the page. If a user has image loading disabled on their browser, they will see the ALT text instead.

ALT text should be concise but descriptive. From an SEO perspective, try to include the page keyword (or a close variation), but not if this sacrifices clarity for disabled users. One keyword is enough - there is no need to stuff in as many as you can, and you could receive a penalty for over-optimising (a practise known as keyword stuffing). Let's look at an example which might appear on a Taekwondo club's programme page or homepage:

GOOD:

Young woman in uniform stands in a Taekwondo ready stance

OR

Young woman stands in a Taekwondo ready stance

BAD:

Taekwondo

Taekwondo student

Person

There are various other ways you could describe this image, depending on how specific you want to be. The above example gives a clear impression of the image, for screen-reader users and for search engines, and we've included the keyword "Taekwondo". Avoid one or two-word descriptions. They rarely convey enough meaning unless the image is something very simple, like your club logo.

To check your site for missing ALT tags, you can either go through them manually in your CMS's image library or by looking at the live page. If you're looking at a live page, hover over the image, right-click and choose "Inspect" (in Chrome). Alternatively, to save time, run a site crawl using the free Screaming Frog SEO Spider software and examine the results shown in the Images tab.

Image filenames

When uploading images to a page, first give them a meaningful file name, preferably including a keyword. Google reads these, so they are a great opportunity to get more of your important context-giving keywords onto the page. For an image of your venue, include the place name as this may help your local search rankings. You should separate words using hyphens or underscores and they should all be in lowercase.

GOOD: taekwondo-student-ready-stance.jpeg

BAD: IMG0037381.JPEG

Image size

Images with large file sizes will slow down your page load speed and harm your search rankings. In fact, bloated images are usually the number one culprit in slowing down a website. To avoid this, it's important to compress images as far as possible, without making them look grainy or blurred.

Website images should be in JPEG, PNG or WebP format. Complex images such as photographs of people work better in JPEG format, whereas something like a logo or illustration works best in PNG. Graphic design tools such as Canva allow you to compress images when you download them. Experiment with how much you can compress an image without the quality noticeably decreasing.

Another way to minimise image sizes is to ensure their dimensions match the space you're placing them in on the page. So, if your image will display in a space 500px wide by 400px tall, resize it in Canva to match. If you upload the same image but the file's dimensions are 1000px x 800px, the page will load more slowly, for zero benefit.

If you don't want to do all this manually, various WordPress plugins are available that will automatically compress your images as you upload them, although the free versions often have limitations.

Some of the best plugins with free tiers include:

- Smush
- Imagify
- ShortPixel.

Action Points

- ☐ Check for missing or un-optimised ALT text.
- ☐ Add descriptive ALT text to all images.
- ☐ Include a keyword where appropriate.
- ☐ Compress your images.

Descriptive URLs

The URL (Uniform Resource Locator) of a page, much like an image filename, should use clear, descriptive text to describe the page and any sub-folders. This helps search engines understand what the page is for. Most CMS do this automatically these days, but it's important to check each page and include the primary keyword. Clear URLs help users understand where they are within your website hierarchy, so it is important for sub-folders (denoted by a forward slash '/') to be unambiguous, too.

Ecommerce websites often suffer from non-descriptive URLs for product pages. If you sell martial arts equipment via an online store, it is worth checking that your URLs describe your products and include keywords.

Let's take an example of an instructor profile page:

https://www.tigermartialarts.com/coaching-team/chief-instructor

Looking at this URL, it is obvious what I am looking at and where the page sits on the website.

Likewise, a location landing page for a single-venue school might look like this:

https://www.tigermartialarts.com/adelaide-lau-gar-kung-fu

In this example, the town, martial art and style keywords are all included. This should send a powerful signal to Google for anyone searching "Lau Gar kung fu classes in Adelaide".

For a multi-venue school or association, the venue pages may exist one level down in the hierarchy, with a general "locations" page inserted between the home page and the individual dojo pages:

https://www.tigermartialarts.com/clubs/adelaide-lau-gar-kung-fu

Whether you refer to your locations as clubs, venues, classes or dojos is up to you.

Other page types

Time-sensitive pages, such as certain blog posts or event/seminar pages, can have their URLs structured in different ways. WordPress allows you to customise how you structure your blog URLs within the Settings > Permalinks screen. By default, the URL includes the publication date. But this makes it more complex, introduces unnecessary sub-folders and gives away the age of your content to Google and to users. This may not be a good thing if you don't post very often.

For new sites, I recommend changing these settings by selecting the "Custom Structure" option on this page and using the following format:

This keeps your blog post addresses clean and tidy whilst still grouping them in a "blog" folder. However, if you already have a well-established blog with lots of posts, it is safer to leave your URL structure alone. Changing it could lead to a drop in rankings and traffic, unless you know how to set up permanent redirects for each post from the old URL to the new one. If not, the risk is greater than the potential reward.

Action Points

- ☐ Use URLs that describe the page.
- ☐ Include the page's primary keyword.
- ☐ Avoid lengthy URLs with lots of sub-folders.
- ☐ Remove dates from your blog URL structure.

7

STRUCTURING YOUR WEBSITE

The pros and cons of a wide vs deep site structure.

Did you know that the way you structure your website can have a big impact on search performance? Well, it can. More to the point, a poorly structured site will allow potential leads to slip away without converting, and that's the last thing you want. Many martial arts school websites look like they were built in the '90s, and seem to be there just to present information, not generate business. After all, I'm a twelfth degree, six-time world champion renowned Grand Master and lineage holder for my obscure system. Everyone must want to learn from me. I don't need to treat my school like a business and promote myself, right? Wrong. Fortunately, you aren't one of these people, as you are reading this book.

Less is more

Many school owners think that "more is more" with their site navigation and content. But it pays to keep navigation as simple as possible. By presenting visitors with too many options, you force them to think too much. As a result, you may lose the opportunity to funnel them down to your programmes and offers, then to your contact form. Psychological studies have shown that the human brain can only hold a certain number of items in working memory at once, your 'RAM', if you will. So, we don't want to overload visitors with too many options on the main navigation menu. As a rule of thumb, aim for seven or fewer main menu links. Nine at the absolute most.

The main website navigation should highlight the most important pages or sections of the site. Pages of secondary importance should have a sub-menu link beneath one of the main sections. Anything else should go into the site footer. As a martial arts school or association, you do not need loads of pages and sections, as your site is there to generate student leads.

The only exceptions to this rule are where you have a Pro Shop or run online training courses. In these cases, I recommend setting up a separate website for the purpose and linking to it. My school had one website aimed at students, and another to run the online Pro Shop, built in Shopify and running on a sub-domain. I linked the two sites to each other, avoiding clutter by trying to cram too much into a single online experience.

Site hierarchy

Website structures (also called the 'information architecture') can be shallow or deep. At one extreme, all pages exist within the root folder, rather than grouped into separate sections/sub-folders. This is a shallow site. At the other extreme, we could use a few site sections with lots of nested sub-folders. This is a deep hierarchy. You should aim for all key information on your website to be accessible to the user within three clicks from the homepage, or from any key landing page. Remember, many, if not most of your users, may enter your site on a page other than your homepage.

The deeper you place a page in your hierarchy, Google will assume the less important it is. After all, if it was important information, it would be high on a main page, wouldn't it?

Here's an example of a shallow but poorly structured site:

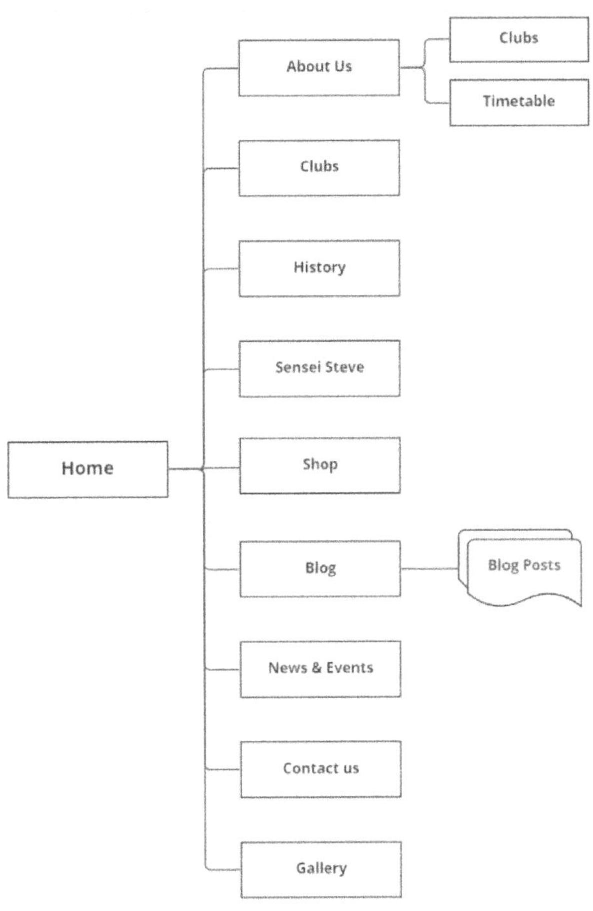

In this example, there is very little structure to the website's information. There are too many links at the top level, creating a confusing user experience.

A poorly structured 'narrow but deep' site might look something like this:

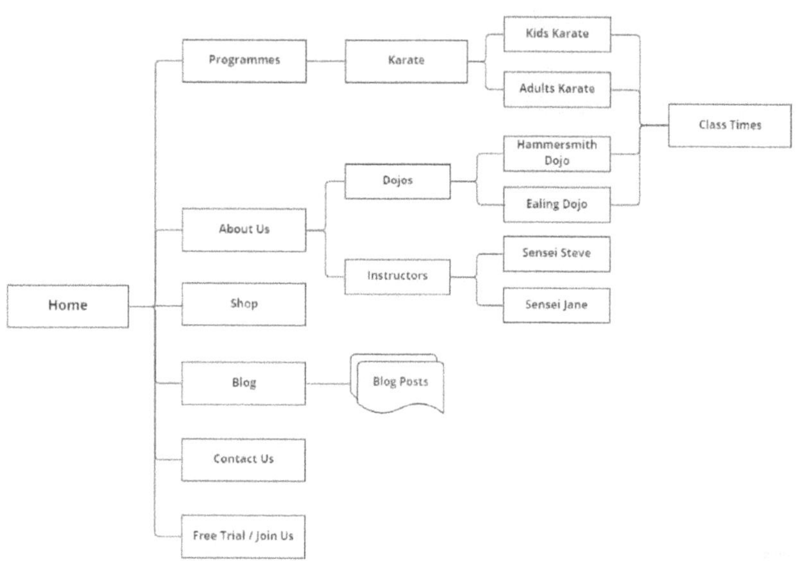

This sort of structure is problematic, as the programme pages "Kids Karate" and "Adults Karate", as well as the location-specific landing pages, are all three clicks away from the domain root. The second-level page "Karate" is unnecessary and serves to dilute the ranking ability of the pages below it. Your most important, high-converting pages containing lead forms should ideally not be further than one or two clicks away from the home page.

Each venue you teach classes at should always have its own page unless they are geographically very close to each other.

Instructors who teach across several towns or distinct areas of a big city should have a page for each location. Combining different locations onto a single venues/dojos page will dilute the local ranking power of that page.

Your ideal site structure will depend very much on the precise nature of your service. When you redesign your site, ask yourself these questions:

1. How many programmes/styles do we offer?
2. How many locations do we teach at?
3. What age groups do we split students into?

The answers to these questions will determine how you ought to structure your site for the best user experience and clarity.

Navigation do's and don'ts

It's tempting to throw everything into the main menu, but always ask yourself the question 'how will this page convert a visitor into a lead?' If the answer is unclear, leave it out. Here are some examples of pages I often see, but advise against including in your main navigation:

- Home (you don't always need this, but ensure your site logo links to your homepage instead)
- Gallery
- Student Login
- Events
- Gradings
- History.

Resources for current students should not appear in the main menu. A members' area link can appear in the site header above the menu, or in the footer or a second-level menu. As an alternative, use a Facebook group to communicate important information to your students. This lets you focus your website only on acquiring new students.

When you have narrowed down what links to include in the main navigation, place them in order of importance. The most important ones should go on the left, or at the top if you're using a vertical menu. Hint: your programme/service pages go first! Less important links can appear further across or down the menu.

Suggested main navigation links (tailored to your school) could include:

- Programmes (or Classes) - if you have more than one or two
- Style name (e.g., Ju-Jitsu)
- Clubs (or Locations/Venues) - if you operate across several sites
- Timetable
- About Us
- Shop
- Blog
- Contact Us / Join Us
- Free Trial (or Trial Offer).

Again, don't use them all, as your menu will become cluttered. Choose what seems most appropriate to your business. For instance, you may choose not to publish your full timetable on one page, to force users to contact you. If you have a single dojo, you don't need a Clubs/Locations page.

Example website structures

Here's an example of a well-structured website for a full-time, multi-style school:

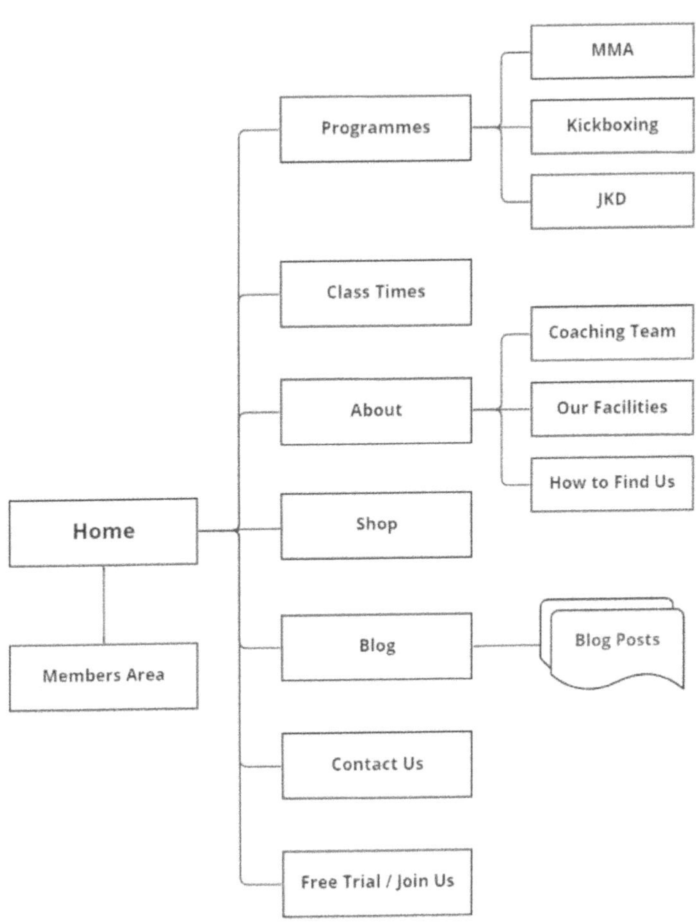

And now an example of a website for a club or association that trains in hired halls in several locations:

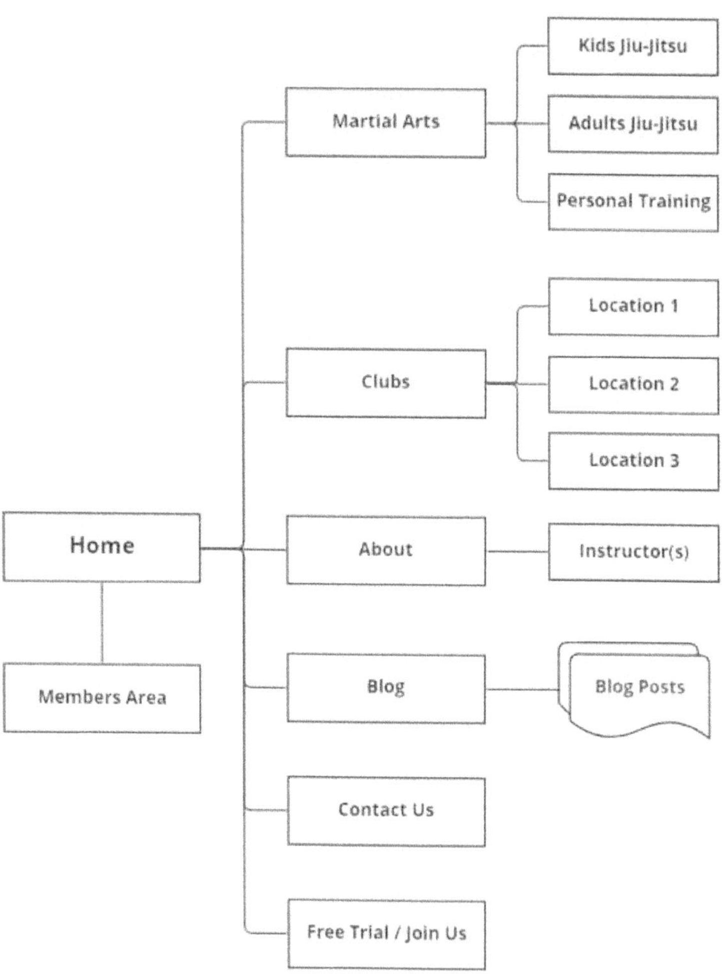

This layout includes a top-level "martial arts" landing page, to cater for most local searches. There are also programme or art specific sub-pages for your martial art-specific keywords.

Each club venue also has its own page, aimed at the specific geographic area each club/class serves.

Site footer

The website footer is the place to include your most important links (again) as well as any secondary pages that don't deserve a place in the main menu. Often these are the legal/compliance related pages. To maximise your local rankings, it's a good idea to include your school's address in the footer of every page, as well as your contact details (phone/email).

There's a growing trend towards bigger website footers. These are often organised into several columns, allowing you to group your links into categories for users. Have separate columns or link lists for:

- Quick Links - listing your programme pages, booking page, timetable.
- Policies / Legal (student charter, photography and video policy, privacy policy, website Ts and Cs, cookie page, etc.).
- Venues - listing all your specific dojo/class/venue pages (if applicable).
- Contact details.
- Any other secondary pages, such as FAQs, special offers, instructors, testimonials, etc.

Other navigation elements

Depending on the design of your website, you may have an area at the very top of the page, above your main menu. This is a great place to display your phone number, email address and links to your social media profiles across every page. Often this information appears above the main menu, or in the footer, or both. You should also have a prominent link or button to your main signup offer page, on every page of your website. Incorporating it into the main menu is usually a good idea.

Internal links

As discussed in the previous chapter, internal links are crucial for providing a seamless user experience. They help Google to understand how your pages relate to each other. If your website has some areas with a deep structure, over two folders down from the root, consider adding internal links from other, more prominent pages. Including internal links will improve the chances of search engine bots crawling these pages and make them easier to find for users.

Mobile responsiveness

To rank at the top of Google, websites should use a "responsive design". This is the term given to the various coding practises which ensure web pages display well on every type of device. Most of your web traffic will be from mobile phones, but it needs to look good across mobile, tablet and desktop. Over the last few years, Google has moved to a "mobile first" index. This means that it determines SERP rankings by looking at how sites perform on mobile devices, rather than how it looks on desktop.

Paying more attention to how your site looks on mobile makes sense for users as well, as most local searches happen on mobile phones. Local searches often have higher buying intent than general ones, as they are more specific, so testing all your core pages on a mobile phone is a great mindset to get into. Load each page on your phone and navigate around, checking that all content, buttons, and images load correctly and are easy to click.

You can test individual pages using Google's Mobile Friendly Test[9].

To monitor the mobile friendliness of your entire website, log into Google Search Console and navigate to the mobile Usability page, under the Experience heading in the menu. This page will give you an overview of which pages Google considers mobile friendly or not. You can drill down further to see more details for any pages that fail this test. Either resolve the issues yourself, or speak to your web developer, as not having a mobile friendly site will count against it in the search results.

[9] https://search.google.com/test/mobile-friendly

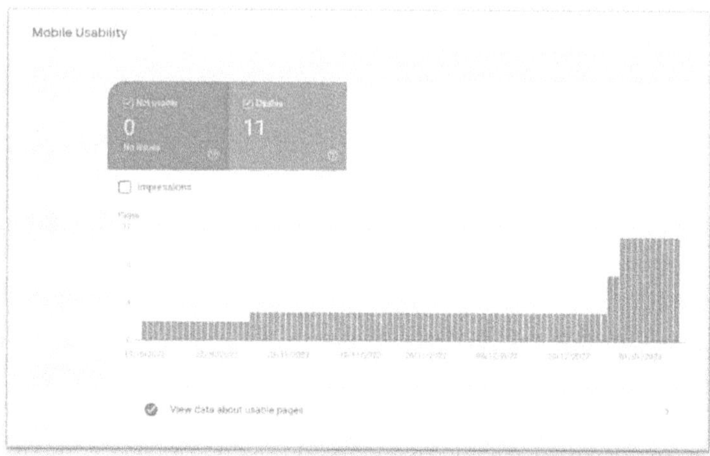

Search Console mobile usability report

A responsive site has other, indirect SEO benefits, in that user engagement (measured by time-on-site and pages per session) will improve, and your bounce rate will decrease, both of which are ranking factors.

To improve your website's mobile friendliness, pay attention to the following considerations.

Fonts

Fonts should be large enough to read on a mobile screen, so normal text should be Size 16, with headings appearing larger. Users don't want to pinch and zoom.

Text

Don't overload your page with lots of text. Users scan and scroll on smartphones, and do not want their screen filled with dense blocks of text. This advice will also help the desktop experience. Break up text with white space, images, and subheadings.

Scrolling

Check that none of your pages have horizontal scrolling, as this can be very annoying for mobile users. Poorly coded tables are often responsible for this. Check over your class timetable and any other tables on your site. Rework them if they do not transform their layout to fit within the visible screen area.

Tap areas

Check that your links and buttons are large enough, and not too close together. Users with big thumbs must be able to tap them without selecting the wrong link by accident.

Load speed

Pages take longer to load on mobile, especially if using a mobile data connection rather than fast Wi-Fi. You can test mobile load speed using the free PageSpeed Insights[10] tool from Google. If a page is slow, consider removing elements and compressing images further. Some content management systems or WordPress page builders allow you to control which sections on a page load for each device type. If you have certain elements on a page that are not essential and slow it down, such as certain images, you may wish to set these not to load for mobile phones. Just remember to test the page afterwards on your devices and check that it still looks good and has a logical flow on mobile.

---

[10] https://pagespeed.web.dev

Technical considerations

Avoid any content or plugins that use iframes to embed content in pages. These rarely display well for mobile phones and can also cause security issues. They are also poor for SEO as bots have difficulty indexing iframed content.

Action Points

- ☐ Map out each page on your site.
- ☐ Categorise pages into a logical structure.
- ☐ Simplify your main menu.
- ☐ Consider footer links to include.
- ☐ Check each page is mobile responsive.

8

SITE SPEED

Tips and techniques to help your pages load faster.

A website's speed is one of the many factors Google and other search engines' algorithms consider when deciding how to order their results. We all know that slow-loading websites are annoying, and we've all got frustrated after only a few seconds and clicked away to another site. Think for a moment about the last time you did this. Chances are, it was today.

Search engines know we are an impatient bunch. In their quest to present us with the fastest answer to our questions and the best experience possible, they favour websites that load fast. Site speed has become ever more important in recent years, as mobile phones have become the dominant devices for browsing. Web pages load more slowly on mobile than on desktop, yet Google's index is now "mobile first". The way your website loads and displays on a phone is what Google looks at first when deciding where you will rank for a search. Google uses a measurement framework called "Core Web Vitals", which is a fancy name for three specific site speed metrics which they have decided are important.

These are:

Metric	What does it mean?
Largest Contentful Paint (LCP)	The time it takes for the web browser to load the largest "thing" visible on the screen, for example, an image or video player.
First Input Delay (FID)	How long it takes for the browser to respond when a user takes their first action on the page, e.g., clicks on a link or button.
Cumulative Layout Shift (CLS)	A layout shift is when something on a web page moves as the page is being loaded. CLS measures the total shift of all elements on a page and gives them a score. Layout shift is bad, because it prevents users from interacting with the page properly until it fully loads.

There are various other metrics used in calculating site speed, such as TTFB (time to first byte). You don't need to understand the minutiae of all these, just that a fast-loading website may give you an edge over your competitors in the search results.

How do I know how fast my website loads?

There are several free tools you can use to check your site's speed score:

- GTmetrix - www.gtmetrix.com
- Pingdom - www.pingdom.com

- PageSpeed Insights - https://pagespeed.web.dev.

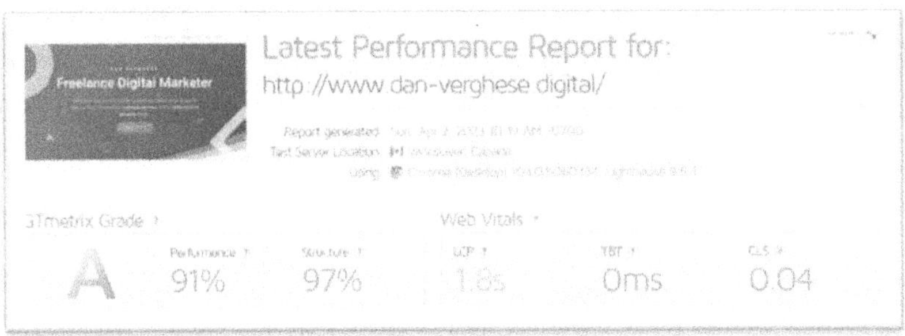

GTmetrix speed report

My favourite is GTmetrix. It gives you a detailed breakdown of how your site loads and helps you diagnose any elements on your site that are causing slowness. PageSpeed Insights is also great and reports separately on loading times for Mobile and Desktop, with a detailed breakdown of Core Web Vitals performance. It also provides detailed recommendations on what you need to do to speed up your site, broken down into four categories:

- Performance
- Accessibility
- Best Practices
- SEO.

Pick one of these tools and run your domain name through it and see what it says. If you are scoring below a B/C on GTmetrix or below about 60% for mobile on PageSpeed Insights, or your site takes over three seconds to load, you need to act.

Simple steps for speeding up your site

Follow the steps below to get your site loading at light-speed. Some of these are more technical than others, so you may need to enlist the help of a web developer. But even if you only focus on the easier ones, you should see big results. The advice below is geared towards WordPress as this is by far the most prevalent CMS on the web today, but the general principles apply to any website, regardless of platform.

Compress and re-size images

Large image file sizes are usually the number one culprit for a slow-loading web page.

Website image files should be under 250KB, so if you have high-resolution images from your site that were not compressed and re-sized before uploading, deal with them as your top priority. On WordPress, various image compression plugins exist, or you can use online graphic design software such as Canva to achieve the same thing.

First, resize an image to the same size that it displays on your web page. There's no need for a 2000-pixel wide image file, if the space it will occupy on the page is only 300 pixels. Resize them to fit the exact dimensions they will occupy, or as close as possible. Avoid going too small, as the image will then become stretched as it loads and will lose quality.

Once resized, download the image as a JPEG, PNG or WEBP, and compress the quality as much as possible without the image becoming blurry or grainy. Now compare the file size of your new image to the original. It should be much smaller.

Upload the compressed image to your website, clear your cache (more on this below) then retest your page's load time to see the impact. There are various third-party plugins available for WordPress which will compress your images as you upload them. If you want to save time, consider using one of these. You will probably need to pay a licence fee, as most of the free versions have limited functionality.

Reduce the number of images or videos

Photos and videos are usually the slowest things on a page to download, as they have the largest file sizes. If you have a web page with a slow load time that is very heavy in images and/or videos, consider removing a few, or reducing their size. Video takes a long time as the browser must load the video player, then stream the video file. Consider whether you *really* need them all on the page. If some images don't add any value, take them out, so long as you do not leave your page feeling very text heavy.

Simplify pages

If you have complicated page layouts or fancy animations and transition effects, think about whether you need them. Complex pages are harder for readers to scan and may be off-putting, and they involve more code behind the scenes to make them work. This increases the page's file size and load time.

Remove or compress background video

Some sites use video clips that auto-play within the homepage header (or 'hero banner'). This can look slick and impressive, but it comes at the cost of significantly slowing down your page. Either use a shorter video clip that loops seamlessly and compress the video more heavily (without noticeably sacrificing quality) or replace it with a static image if you find your load time suffering.

Minify your CSS, HTML and JavaScript

'Minification' is a technical term that refers to squashing the CSS, HTML and JavaScript code that lives in the background and makes your pages work, making it shorter and therefore load faster. Minification involves removing all comments and blank spaces from code, as well as other changes which reduce the number of characters required to describe the page in code. This, in turn, reduces the page's file size.

You don't really need to know how it works, but if you have a web developer, ask them to minify your website's code. There are many WordPress optimisation plugins that will do this for you, but be warned, it is possible to break your site if you are not careful. Take a site backup first and only tinker with these settings if you know what you are doing. Otherwise, leave it to your developer. Minifying scripts is one of the most common, and most effective, ways to speed up your site.

Update your plugins, themes and software

Regularly update all the software that underpins your website, including the core software (e.g. WordPress), unless you are using a subscription service that does all this for you. WordPress sites require regular updates of the content management system, the theme your site uses, and the various plugins which provide you with extended features and functions. For example, your contact form probably uses a plugin, as does your backup solution, image gallery, booking system, etc. Plugin developers regularly find bugs in their products and release new versions to correct them. Keeping plugins up to date is beneficial from a security perspective, but it also helps to prevent your site from slowing down through outdated code.

Remove unnecessary plugins

Plugins are extra pieces of software that plug into your CMS to give you extra features and functions, and are common in WordPress sites, as well as some other content management systems. Deactivate any you aren't using anymore. Test that your site still works as expected, then delete them. This should speed up your website, as less code is running in the background.

You can also try turning off plugins one at a time and re-testing your page load speeds, to see if a specific plugin is slowing the site down. If you find any that are, consider replacing the plugin with a more efficient, lightweight alternative.

Enable caching

'Caching' is a process whereby a web page pre-loads on the web server in advance, then delivered to a user's web browser in an 'already assembled' state, rather than being put together as you try to load the page. Think of a furniture analogy - a non-cached page is like an IKEA flat-pack. It will take some time to put together before you can see the finished product, whereas if a fully assembled table is delivered to your home, you can enjoy it faster and with less effort. Caching plugins assemble your pages in advance, which makes them load faster.

Once you have caching set up on your site, any changes you make to the content may not show up straight away, so remember to delete the cache if you cannot see your latest edits on the live site. You can do this from within the plugin.

Clean up your database

Every website has a database behind it that stores information about all the elements that make up the site. Over time, and as websites develop, these databases can become bloated and inefficient. You can install plugins that will check your database and tidy it up for you. You can also manually delete spam comments or any unnecessary files, such as old image files in the media library.

Update PHP

If your website runs on PHP (a server-side programming language), as all WordPress websites do, ensure you are using the latest stable version of the code. Newer versions are more efficient and lead to faster loading. To find out which is the latest, stable version that your site can run on, log a ticket with your web hosting company and ask their support team. They will let you know, and can either update your PHP version for you, or will explain how you can do it yourself. Always take a full backup first!

Switch hosting providers

Some web hosting companies are better than others. Most martial arts websites do not require vast server resources as your site will be relatively low traffic. Whilst you could upgrade your hosting package, it may be worth switching to a new hosting company that has a better setup. The cheapest web hosting plans are almost always 'shared hosting', which means your website is competing for resources with lots of other websites running from the same servers. Some hosting companies have much faster server setups and superior caching, meaning your site will load faster without you having to shell out more money for an upgraded plan.

Switch to a lightweight theme

Some website themes require more processing power and involve a lot more code behind the scenes than others. Do some research online and see if you can switch to a more lightweight theme. This will necessitate redesigning your website, so is best done when you are already planning a redesign.

Don't host your own videos

Downloading and streaming videos consumes a lot of bandwidth and processing power. Don't upload your video files directly to your website or server. Instead, host them on a video streaming service such as YouTube or Vimeo. Then embed the video into your web page using the streaming platform's embed code, or whatever video player widget comes with your website. But even though your videos are now hosted elsewhere, try not to use more than one per page, as they will still slow down your website.

On a positive note, embedding video can help your SEO in other ways. By embedding a short video on your home page or on your programme pages, you will reduce the bounce rate and improve 'dwell time' (the time users remain on your site) for your pages. This tells search engines that visitors are finding your website useful, because they are staying and interacting with it rather than immediately leaving, or 'bouncing off'. This can positively affect your rankings, so use video, but sparingly and carefully.

Use a Content Delivery Network (CDN)

CDNs such as Cloudflare are third-party services you can subscribe to, which act like a caching plugin, hosting copies of your websites on servers around the world. Wherever a user is hitting your site from, the CDN will direct their browser to download the cached version from the geographically closest servers, thus reducing load time. Cloudflare has a free tier, which can be worth using if you struggle to speed your website up in other ways.

Of course, as a martial arts school owner, you only really need your site to load quickly within a few miles' radius of your dojo, unless you offer online training resources. When choosing a hosting provider, try to find out where their servers are located. Ensure your website will be hosted in the same country as you are. A UK school hosting its website on data centres in the USA is not doing itself any favours with load time.

Eliminate redirects

Over time, as websites grow and change, they can sometimes accumulate redirects. Perhaps you took down some old web pages and replaced them at some point, redirecting the URLs to the new page. In the worst case, redirect chains can occur, where a URL is redirected to another, which in turn is redirected to another. This slows down your website loading speed, as the browser must try each URL before reaching the actual page and loading it. If you have redirected pages, update any internal links to point directly to the correct web address, bypassing any redirects. This keeps your links simple and tidy and will help your SEO.

There are plenty of other ways to speed up a website, but most of them are very technical and require an experienced developer, or need to be factored in when you first build your website. But if you address some of the factors above, starting with compressing images and then working your way down, you'll see clear improvements. If you can get your website to load consistently in less than a couple of seconds, you're doing well.

Action Points

- ☐ Check your website's load time.
- ☐ Work out what factors are slowing your site down.
- ☐ Fix speed issues one by one e.g. compress images.
- ☐ Re-test your load time.
- ☐ Fix the next issue.
- ☐ Rinse and repeat.

9

PERMISSION TO LAND

Optimising your landing pages.

Your main landing pages are some of the most important content on your website, and you should prioritise them when conducting SEO. But what exactly do we mean by 'landing page'? A website's key landing pages are those pages on the site which explain your products and services, and which you want visitors to arrive at first.

Most of your search visitors may well land on your home page, but many businesses find other pages rank higher than their home page does. Home pages must be all things to all people, providing signposts to everything a business or organisation does. Because of this, they are often unfocussed. Home pages are difficult to optimise for specific keyword searches with high buyer intent, so instead they act as a shop window to your brand. Often, it is best to get more specific pages about products, services, or programmes to rank as well. Users may then skip the homepage and find what they are looking for straight from search results, without having to navigate within a site.

We also use landing pages as destinations for organic or paid marketing campaigns. For example, a Google or Facebook ads campaign should funnel users to a landing page which matches the content of the ads and fulfils the user's need. Campaign landing pages are often not part of the main website. They sit apart as standalone pages, so that users can see no links or other content that may distract them from the campaign's call to action.

The most important landing pages on a martial arts school owner's website are:

1. Location pages (assuming you teach at more than one location).
2. Programme pages.

Choose your target keywords

Each landing page should target one specific keyword. All your optimisation effort should go towards getting the page to rank for that keyword, which is then also likely to rank for other variations of the keyword and attract further visitors. The keyword for an MA school's programme pages should include your geographic location.

For example, Tai Chi classes for senior citizens may have a dedicated programme page, targeting the keyword "Liverpool Tai Chi". The page will describe the classes in more detail than the site's homepage.

Keyword optimisation

The keyword "Liverpool Tai Chi" should appear in the page's meta title tag and within the meta description. It should also appear in the first paragraph (preferably the first sentence) on the page, and within the main page heading, which is defined by the <H1></H1> HTML tag.

The landing page should include several distinct sections. Each section should have its own sub-heading, which can include keyword variations. In this example, we could break the page into the following sections:

- What is Tai Chi?
- What are the health benefits of Tai Chi?
- 70+ Liverpool Tai Chi classes
- Tai Chi in Sefton Park.

Each of these sections should have a sub-heading using an H2 or H3 tag, which provides Google, and users, with more context around the service provided. The sub-headings include supporting keywords and location signals (Sefton Park is a major park in Liverpool).

Location signals

Include your NAP (name, address, and phone number) on every landing page, using a consistent format across pages. Ensure that this format matches that of your Google Business Profile and other business listing citations.

You should also embed on the page a Google map showing a pin of your precise location – either your dojo or the halls you hire for your classes. Proximity is one of the biggest ranking factors in local search. Pinning your location in Google Maps and including it on a page helps search engines to surface your site to people searching close by.

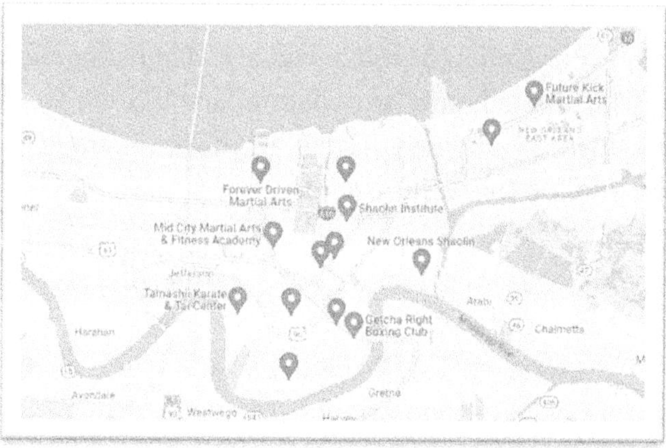

Pinned martial arts school locations in New Orleans

As well as the map, include a "how to find us" section with directions to your class. Within this text, refer to key landmarks in the vicinity. You may also wish to mention or provide links to other local attractions or amenities at the bottom of the page. All these factors strengthen the location signals you are sending Google, whilst also helping your potential new recruits to find your class.

Calls to action

Every landing page, whether it is marketing a specific programme or a location page, should have a single, primary call to action (CTA). A call to action is the thing that we want all our visitors to do when they land on a page.

Types of CTA used by businesses and organisations include:

- Clicking a button or link (e.g., to a contact us page, online booking system, or further information on the topic).
- Filling in a contact form.
- Downloading a document.
- Watching an embedded video.
- Signing up to a mailing list.
- Picking up the phone to call the business.
- Logging into or signing up for an account.
- Purchasing a product (adding to basket).
- Making a donation.

As an MA school website should focus on lead generation, the primary CTA of your landing pages should ask your users to fill in the contact form. Embed the contact form on the same page, rather than using a button leading to a separate contact page. If your landing pages do not have embedded forms, consider redesigning them. On-page forms reduce the number of clicks a user needs to make and increase your conversion rate.

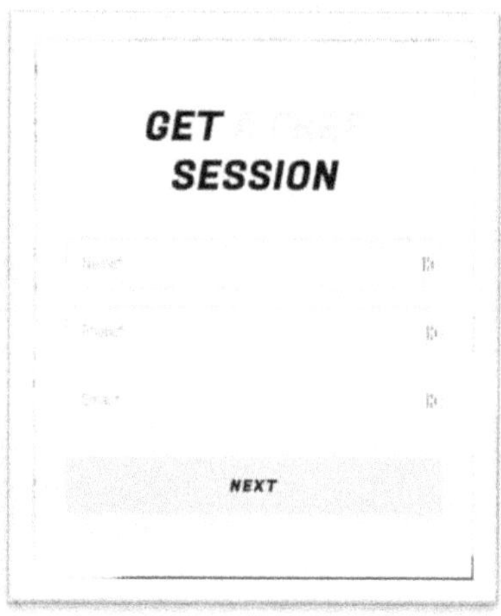

Lead generation forms should preferably appear near the top of the page, or 'above the fold', as it is sometimes called. The further someone must scroll, the less likely they are to see it and fill it in. If you have a form near the top of the page, repeat it near the bottom for users who scroll down to read your page content before deciding to get in touch. Or you could use a sticky sidebar that is always visible as the user scrolls down.

This is a design decision for which there isn't a right or wrong answer. I recommend split testing this to find the layout that converts best for your page. Try one layout for a month and track how many leads come in from this specific page. Then, the following month, move the form or otherwise change the page layout, and review your results at the end of month two. For those with bigger budgets, specialist split testing (also called A/B testing) software is available. This will be overkill for most MA schools, given the low-traffic nature of most local business websites.

Example flow for a programme landing page

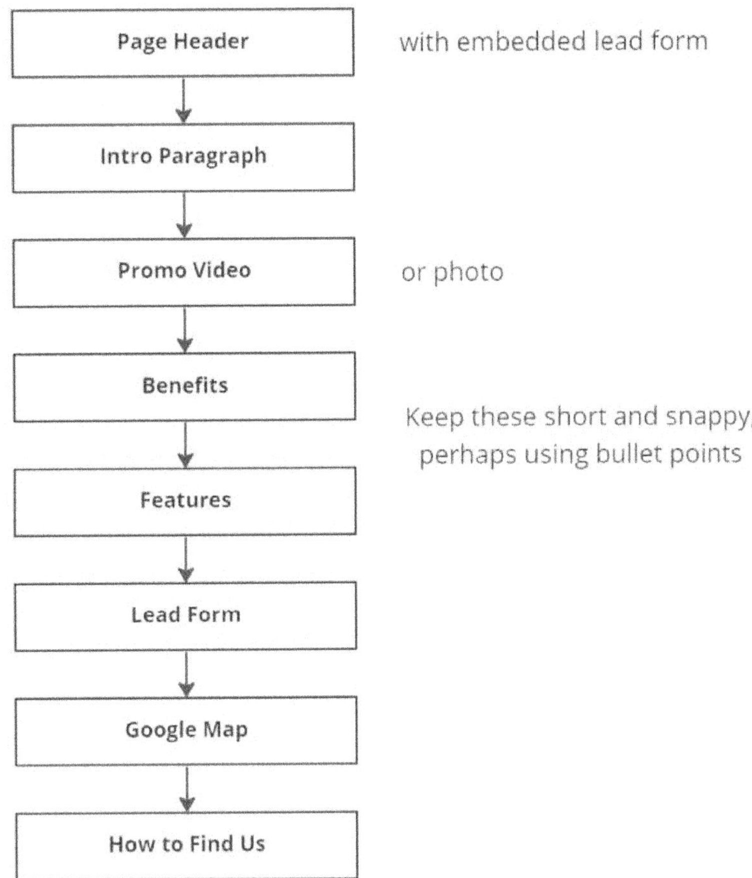

Form design

Whilst not an SEO issue, consider your lead form design. Asking for too much information from a user will probably decrease the number of leads you gain via the website. Keep it quick, easy, and minimal, asking only for:

- Name
- Email address
- Phone number
- Comment.

You may also want to include check boxes or a drop-list asking which specific programme they are enquiring about (i.e., adults or kids, or the name of the art if you run a multi-style school). However, by using a separate form on each landing page, you can remove the need for this. Name the form appropriately in your CMS so that you know where the enquiry has come from. If you use school management software with CRM (customer relationship management) functionality, you may be able to embed forms generated by your software onto your web page. This will automate the lead acquisition process and remove manual steps, as leads will appear in your account immediately.

Visual elements

Video

To make your landing page as engaging and easy to understand as possible, consider embedding a promotional video, if you have one. Video has now become the dominant format online. A good-quality short film that shows your students having fun and showcases your facilities can help your conversion rate.

Video also has an SEO benefit. Whilst Google cannot yet understand the contents of a film, when users watch a video, they are engaging with the page and spending more time on it.

As a result, Google will see the page as more engaging. If you don't already have them, consider creating programme-specific videos, ideally under two minutes long. The video itself, if made public on YouTube, may even rank in its own right. Pay close attention to writing a detailed and effective video description, and to your choice of keywords when publishing your videos on YouTube. Include relevant links to your website in the video description. These steps will both optimise the video for users searching within YouTube, and for Google searches. When Google displays a video within search results, they often appear above the normal organic rankings. Well-optimised video can be a great tactic for leapfrogging to the top of the SERPs, and you don't even need to use your website to do it.

Photos

It is always wise to break up blocks of text content on a page with photos, provided they are high-quality and relevant. Remember to compress the file sizes as far as possible without the image quality suffering, so as not to slow down your page load speed.

Try to use photos of your own students and facilities wherever possible, not stock photos. We all know that a picture speaks a thousand words. If students can see what happens in your classes and can imagine themselves joining in, they are more likely to enquire.

All photos embedded within a landing page should have descriptive ALT text, with the page keyword or a close variation of it included. Use a descriptive file name too and include the page keyword in it. On your location or club landing pages, always include a photo of the venue. An exterior photo within the "How to find us" section will help students find the premises for their first class. It also gives you the opportunity to use the venue name in the photo's filename and ALT text, which is valuable from a local search perspective.

Page length

It can be tempting to keep landing pages short and sweet, to minimise clutter and make the lead form as prominent as possible. Google does not rank pages based on their word count, but a page with too few words is unlikely to be comprehensive enough to rank at the top of the results. So, try to include several hundred words on the page, without writing 'fluff' to pad it out.

Summarise the purpose of the page with an introductory paragraph, then cover off the major benefits and features of your programme. Describe what you teach at each venue, providing class times, venue addresses and driving directions. You can also include FAQs and testimonials if you wish.

Action Points

- ☐ Optimise each page for a specific keyword.
- ☐ Use keywords in meta tags and page content.
- ☐ Break up page content with images and video.
- ☐ Include a clear call to action.
- ☐ Provide plenty of location signals on your page.
- ☐ Embed lead forms.

10

CITATIONS – TIME FOR A NAP?

Boost off-page SEO through business listings.

Citations are a key component of Google's local algorithm and should be an important ingredient in your SERP domination strategy. Research in 2021 by BrightLocal found citations were the fourth most important ranking factor for local organic search. They are also the fifth most important factor for whether a website shows in the Local Pack.

What is a citation, anyway?

A citation is not the same thing as a backlink. When we refer to a citation, we mean an instance of your business's name and other key details that are on a third-party website. Usually, these mentions are in the form of a business listing. Citations usually include at least the name, address, and phone number (NAP). They may sometimes contain other useful information, such as opening hours, website address, and social media handles.

Example business listing citation

Why are citations important?

Having lots of citations for your business increases its authority with search engines. The more references there are across the web to a business, the more authority search engines will ascribe it. This may boost a business up the local organic search results or increase the likelihood of it appearing in the Local Pack, above the organic results.

Over the last few years, citations have become less important. Search engines have become more sophisticated at working out which websites best answer a user's search intent. Other factors, like geographic proximity, have become more important in determining local rankings. But citations serve a triple purpose - not only do they boost a site's rankings, they also often rank high in SERPs in their own right. When looking at my own school's local rankings, I found that for many important keywords, my business listings actually outranked my site's programme and location pages. For some terms, I was dominating page one of Google by taking up to **seven** of the available places!

This almost total lock-out of page one was a combination of:

- Home page
- Programme page
- Social media profiles (e.g., Facebook business page)
- Several business listing citations.

For other keywords, my site's pages ranked below some third-party citations, particularly local business listings or local council pages. Were it not for these citations, I may not have appeared on page one for some of those keywords. Also, some business directories drive referral traffic and generate leads. Users can discover your club via a third-party listing like Yelp or Yell, then click through to your site or contact you straight from the listing.

Not all citations are equal. Some business listing sites are spammy and are best avoided, as they could lower your site's authority. Many ask for payment for backlinks, but in most cases, you shouldn't pay for links. Purchasing links is not only against Google's terms of service, but the cost can mount up and outweigh any benefit, given how many business listings are out there.

Is citation building different from backlink building?

Yes, although the two are often lumped together, they are slightly different. Backlink building is the practise of obtaining relevant hyperlinks from authoritative, relevant sites, back to your own. Citations are instances where a business' name appears on another website. They are more of a numbers game - we want our school's name and contact details to appear on as many sites as possible. If a business listing offers a free backlink, you should of course take advantage of it, but link-less citations are still valuable.

Types of citation

- Third-party national / international business directories
- Local or region-specific business directories
- Social media mentions, e.g. Facebook pages
- Your Google Business Profile
- Industry/sector specific directories
- Local council business listing pages
- Other local business listings such as local newspaper sites, Chambers of Commerce
- Review sites
- Bing Maps.

Take a NAP

When building citations, NAP is king:

Name

Address

Phone Number

At the least, you want to add these three pieces of information to business directories. Consistency is king, so before starting your citation building campaign, decide exactly what format your NAP will take. Enter the NAP exactly the same way for all listings and match them with what appears on your website and Google Business Profile. Google needs to understand that each citation is referencing the same business entity, so you can make it easier to understand this by using the same format everywhere.

For example, +44 7392062839 is not the same as 0739206839.

25 Pork Pie St. is not the same as 25 Pork Pie Street.

Pick one format and standardise it across all listings.

Citation building process

There are two main approaches you can take to building your citations. Manual, or automated. Various local SEO tools exist in the market, which are designed to auto-submit your NAP to many of the biggest listing sites. They can save time but come at a cost. For most dojos, I recommend taking a manual approach. But if you operate a chain of schools across many locations, you may have the scale and incentive to invest in a software tool to do this for you.

Examples of software that will submit and manage your directory listings are:

- BrightLocal
- Semrush
- Moz Local
- Whitespark.

These services take the pain out of local citation management, but usually only connect to the major national or international directories. They will miss the hyper-local or industry-specific directories that may in fact be of most value to your club.

Business listing directories come and go, but at the time of writing, these are some of the international ones:

2findlocal - www.2findlocal.com
Apple Maps
Bing Places for Business - www.bingplaces.com
Brownbook - brownbook.net
Centralindex - gb.centralindex.com
Cybo - www.cybo.com
Enroll Business - gb.enrollbusiness.com
FindGlocal - www.findclocal.com
Infobel - www.infobel.com
Lacartes - www.lacartes.com
Local Gyms & Fitness - www.localgymsandfitness.com
Mapquest - www.mapquest.com
Yell - yell.com

UK business directories

Britaine - www.britaine.co.uk
Business Rank - www.businessrank.co.uk
Cylex - www.cylex-uk.co.uk
Freeindex - www.freeindex.co.uk
Fyple - www.fyple.co.uk
Hotfrog - www.hotfrog.co.uk
Just Landed - www.justlanded.co.uk
Locanto - www.locanto.co.uk
My Local Services - www.mylocalservices.co.uk

Opendi - www.opendi.co.uk
Real People Media - www.realpeoplemedia.co.uk
Scoot - www.scoot.co.uk
Thebestof - thebestof.co.uk
The Independent Directory - directory.independent.co.uk
Thetradefinder - www.thetradefinder.co.uk
Thomsonlocal - www.thomsonlocal.com
UK Small Business Directory - www.uksmallbusinessdirectory.co.uk
Yalwa - www.yalwa.co.uk
Yelp - yelp.com / yelp.co.uk

US business directories

Better Business Bureau - www.bbb.org
Merchant Circle - www.merchantcircle.com
Nextdoor Business - business.nextdoor.com
Yellowbook - www.yellowbook.com
Yellow Pages - www.yellowpages.com

There are too many US-based business directories to list in full here, plus directories at state and local level. Do your research online and draw up a target list that is most relevant to where your club is based.

Martial Arts specific directories

Dojos.co.uk (UK-based directory of MA clubs)
Dojos.info (US equivalent of dojos.co.uk)
Get Into Martial Arts - getintomartialarts.com (UK-based club directory for NEST Management Ltd clients)
Martial Art Experts - www.martialartexperts.co.uk

Safeguarding Code in Martial Arts - safeguardingcode.com (UK-based safeguarding organisation which has a map-based listing of certified clubs)

Start with Yelp and Yell. These are two of the largest and most authoritative directories on the Internet. If you have more than one venue, create separate listings for each. Before creating a new listing, first check that you do not already have one. It is possible that you or a colleague have set one up in the past, or that listing data on one site has already been pulled in from another. Some business listings take their data from other aggregator sites, so by submitting yourself to an aggregator, you will appear on a range of similar listings elsewhere on the web.

In the US, the big aggregator sites include:

Data Axle - local-listings.data-axle.com/search
Foursquare - www.foursquare.com
Neustar Localeze - www.neustarlocaleze.biz/small-business-services

So, if you are US-based, get yourself listed on these three sites as early as possible.

I found that the local category pages on dojos.co.uk rank well for certain keywords. On the downside, they list all clubs in a local area, so users will see a list of your competitors too. However, provided you have a place on the list, you won't be at a disadvantage. Your club's details will be visible to potential students who are looking for schools in your area. Dojos.co.uk club listings are free, but they charge for a backlink.

I recommend not paying for this, as it's the citation we want here.

To start your citation building campaign, finalise your NAP, and create a paragraph or two that describes your school, as some listings allow you to add a bit of descriptive text. Include a few of your top keywords within the description. Then, create a tracking spreadsheet. This will act as a central reference point when you need to update your business details in the future.

The spreadsheet should include the following fields:

- Directory site name
- Directory site login page URL
- URL to your specific listing
- Username
- Password
- Backlink? (Y/N).

Of course, you can add further fields or change these to suit you, but you should at least record what listings you have, where to find them, and how to log back in to amend them. If you have a team member to do this for you or if you contract the work out to someone, this is even more important. You do not want to risk being locked out of your listings and unable to keep your details current. For example, if you move venues or change your opening hours.

Once you have worked through all the big global listing sites, add your school to all the national sites for your country. The list above is UK-centric, so do some research to find the most appropriate sites to use if you are outside the UK.

When you've ticked all these off, search for listings specific to your state, county, or even town. It is likely that you'll find some local sites offering free listings, so take advantage of them. Their geographic proximity to you may give them a greater relevance score in Google's algorithm. Then, search for any other martial arts, sports clubs, or gym-specific directories in your country. If you operate a full-time martial arts gym, you can take advantage of various gym directories on health and fitness websites.

If you're building your citations by hand, it is best to take your time and only do a few each week, for two reasons. First, it's a soul-crushingly tedious job, so give yourself a break and spread it out. Second, search engines respond best to authority and references that accrue over time. This looks more natural rather than lots of listings popping up at once, as the product of a concerted campaign by a business owner. This is true for citations, backlinks, and customer reviews. In SEO, a steady drip is preferable to a sudden deluge.

Advanced citation building

If you are lucky enough to have access to a professional SEO tool such as Semrush, there are other methods you can use to identify citation and backlinking opportunities. Using Semrush's Backlink Gap tool, you can enter up to five competitors (ideally large, popular, and well-established schools in your locality or region), then analyse their backlinks. The tool will identify which domains are linking to them and not to your own site. This exercise will help to identify other listing sites you may not have been aware of. You can then approach them and ask for a business citation or a backlink.

Unstructured citations

An unstructured citation is a mention of your business online that is not within a directory listing. It could appear on any site and may not contain the full name, address and phone number, or your promotional blurb. Unstructured citations can arise from:

- Local press coverage
- Websites of teams you sponsor
- Social media mentions
- Blog posts and comments
- Forum posts
- Supplier websites, etc.

Unstructured citations are harder to get than structured ones. You have less direct control over them, as they usually rely on someone wanting to talk about your business. PR campaigns can help you gain this type of citation.

Action Points

- ☐ Define the exact format of your NAP.
- ☐ Create a tracking spreadsheet.
- ☐ Create a target list of websites.
- ☐ Work down your list, creating listings on each site.
- ☐ Review your citations every 6-12 months.

11

BACKLINK TO THE FUTURE

Strategies for obtaining backlinks and growing site authority.

Backlink building is the process of persuading other websites to link to your website. They are also one of the most important ranking factors, as when a site links to your content, it is giving a vote of confidence that your site is worth visiting. All things being equal, the more backlinks a site can get, the better it will rank.

The best backlinks to get are from popular, prestigious websites that themselves rank high in search and have lots of their own backlinks. When one site links to another, it transfers link equity (sometimes called 'link juice') to the target page. This increases the authority of that page with search engines. There are two types of links:

- "dofollow" links
- "nofollow" links.

A "dofollow" link is a standard, normal hyperlink from one page to another. Googlebot can crawl these links as normal. However, "nofollow" links are so called because they include a piece of code in the link's HTML tag, which reads:

rel="nofollow". This code tells Googlebot to ignore the link and not to follow it. As such, "nofollow" links have no *direct* SEO value, as link equity does not flow through them. All links on Wikipedia are "nofollow" links, to prevent people from gaming the site to boost their own rankings.

"Dofollow" links are the most important for rankings, and amassing good quality links will help a website's pages to rise in the rankings. "Nofollow" links are still valuable though. They may still lead visitors to your site, increasing your traffic, engagement, and potential for generating leads. Ideally, a website should have a mixture of both types of links, for a 'natural backlink profile' that does not look suspicious to search engines.

Building local links

Building links to your martial art school website can be difficult. For a local business, the best links to get are from other businesses in your general locality. Local business listings can be a source of these if they allow you to include a link without paying (see the Citations chapter).

It's time to get creative and think about how to forge connections with other businesses, with the aim of free publicity and a backlink.

Potential linkers could include:

- Suppliers of equipment you use
- The websites of venues you regularly hire
- Sports teams you sponsor
- Your students' own sites, if they have them

- Local businesses
- The local Chamber of Commerce
- Local newspapers and blogs
- Local radio websites.

Equipment suppliers

Think about who you buy your martial arts equipment from, particularly if they are a small or local supplier. Would they be willing to link to your site in exchange for a positive testimonial or case study? If you use a local company to print your branding onto uniforms or other merchandise, it may be worth approaching them. Large, national suppliers are less likely to go for this tactic.

Venue websites

Community halls and sports centres often list regular hirers on their websites, so don't miss a trick and reach out to your contact there. I ran classes at a purpose-built martial arts centre as one of many hirers, but they agreed to list my school on their website, with a logo and backlink. This generated leads, as well as a valuable, relevant backlink for SEO purposes.

Sponsorships

Run a Google search for "location + sponsorships" and browse the results. You'll probably find local sports teams or players who you could sponsor, for a moderate sum. Depending on your budget, you may be able to get your school's branding added to the team kit, or you could sponsor an individual player. Check with the team that you will receive a backlink from their site in return, before committing. Sponsorships can be a great marketing tactic, apart from the potential SEO value.

Student websites

Some of your existing students may be business owners or sole traders. They might be prepared to link to you, in exchange for promoting their services to other students on your Facebook Group or email newsletter.

Local businesses

Think about whether there are any other local businesses you are on good terms with who might link to you. This could be in exchange for giving their staff a membership discount or promoting their services to your students.

Chamber of Commerce

In the UK, the Chambers of Commerce[11] provides a membership body in each town for local businesses to join and network, usually for a modest annual fee. Often, one benefit of membership is the ability to list your business on their website. Consider joining your local chamber as you may well benefit from it in other ways too. If you live in another country, check out the local equivalent.

Local newspapers and blogs

Local newspapers usually have an online version and may operate their own local business listings. Otherwise, use your PR skills to reach out to the sports reporter and invite them

---

[11] https://www.britishchambers.org.uk/page/join-a-chamber

along to your school. Consider what newsworthy events you can run. Charity fundraisers, such as a “kickathon” or “throwathon” could attract local media coverage. At the very least, getting your school’s name in the paper is good public relations and will provide an unstructured citation. You may also gain a backlink from the online version of the news article.

Local bloggers can also be a good potential source of links. Bloggers are always looking for new content, so do some online research and reach out to any local blogs that look active. For example, a blog focussing on local activities for children or families may be open to a guest post or interview, gaining you a backlink in the process.

Local radio

If you can grab yourself a guest spot on a local radio station, you’ll have the opportunity to talk about the benefits of martial arts for adults and children in your area. The station will promote your appearance on their website and social media. I did this for my school and enjoyed it. The radio station published the recording as a podcast, which I embedded in a blog post on my site afterwards, for extra marketing value.

HARO

HARO (Help A Reporter Out)[12] is an online service where you can subscribe to receive email alerts from journalists. Journalists use it to find experts to quote in their stories. If you can monitor these alerts and provide timely, insightful

[12] www.helpareporter.com

opinions, your submission may be included in their piece. It can gain you a mention in articles ranging from niche publications to national newspapers and well-known magazines.

It's hard work and results do not come immediately, but this can be a useful tactic to gain unstructured citations and backlinks from authoritative sites. Don't forget to include your website URL with your pitch, as well as any other information the journalist is asking for.

Specialist martial arts websites

If you are a well-known figure with interesting things to say about martial arts or combat sports, you might write for specialist martial arts websites or magazines. Any backlinks gained through this approach are likely to be valuable, as popular special interest sites are likely to have higher domain authority than your own website. You will also raise your profile within the industry, which can have many other benefits.

Backlink analysis

If you have access to a professional SEO tool like Semrush, you can use the Backlink Analytics Tool to discover all the domains that link to your competitors or to other popular martial arts school sites. Comb this list and identify any websites that might also be willing to link to you. This is also a great way to find business directories for you to submit your company to and earn a structured citation. The Link Gap Analysis tool will show domains linking to your competitors, but not to you. Reach out to any that look relevant and reputable.

For a free alternative, check out Ahrefs' Backlink Checker[13] to find out what sites are linking to your popular competitors. You can then investigate to see whether there are any opportunities to get a link from them yourself.

Action Points

- ☐ Research local businesses to partner with.
- ☐ Find local lifestyle/activities blogs and reach out.
- ☐ Contact local media outlets.
- ☐ Ask your existing contacts for backlinks.
- ☐ Sign up for HARO alerts.

13 https://ahrefs.com/backlink-checker

12

KILLER CONTENT

Content marketing strategies for success.

Content marketing is one of the most effective and popular marketing strategies in use today, across most industries. It is an "inbound marketing" approach that seeks to attract customers to your business via exciting, engaging, and informative content. It is the opposite of outbound marketing (read – Facebook and Google ads) which most martial arts schools are familiar with. Inbound marketing pulls customers in via great content. Outbound marketing interrupts customers where they already are. For a great content marketing strategy, you can combine the two. Create engaging, original content, then amplify your organic reach using targeted ads to promote it. A content marketing approach seeks to:

- Attract website visitors.
- Boost site engagement.
- Build backlinks.

Content marketing can be difficult for martial arts schools which sell a physical, in-person service. But it is possible, and some instructors are killing it with original, interesting output.

Content can be:

Educational

- Short technique breakdowns
- Longer instructional pieces
- Self-defence tips
- Training methods and nutrition
- Interviews with instructors and students
- Articles about the history of your art.

Topical or opinion pieces

- Latest news and goings on in your school
- Competition success stories
- Student of the week/month
- Commentary on recent trends or news stories
- Controversial debates.

Entertaining

- Amusing or light-hearted content
- Show off the personalities in your club
- Memes
- Challenges
- Fancy dress
- Demonstrations.

The subject of content marketing can, and has, filled several books. Here we will concentrate on how content marketing tactics can work together with SEO to generate web traffic.

Blogging

Blogging is one of the longest-lived and most popular content marketing tactics. It is the one which delivers the most SEO value, as text on a web page is easy for search engines to understand. If you decide to blog, it is important to keep up a regular schedule of posting. Think about what a sustainable posting rate would look like for you, and who in your school can write your posts.

Blog posts that attract organic traffic should be on a popular topic, backed up by careful keyword research. Target each post at one or two medium or long-tail keywords (keywords containing several words which are more specific and easier to rank for). There is no "ideal" word count, but they should be lengthy enough to do full justice to the topic.

When crafting a blog post, think about the structure and divide it into smaller sections, each with a keyword-rich subheading using H2 or H3 tags. Break up the wall of text further with high quality, relevant, and original images, with ALT text. Use bulleted lists where possible, to make content easier to scan and introduce more white space. Sentences should be short and simple, with no typos or grammatical mistakes. If spelling and grammar are not your strong point, ask someone else to proof-read your posts before they go up. You could also run them through online writing aids such as Grammarly and Hemingway.

Popular styles of blog post include:

- Predictions and trends
- Interviews
- Listicles (e.g., "the top 5 kicks in taekwondo")
- "How to" posts and tutorials (e.g., how to stretch for a higher side kick)
- Ultimate guides
- Case studies.

As well as the post types above, you can use your blog to report on upcoming or recent events, such as gradings and competitions, or tournament results. Be sure to optimise every post's meta title, description and H1 header for the chosen keyword, and include a link or two to your programme or signup pages. You should also link your post to any related ones already on your site and consider updating those to link back to the new one. This helps to create topical clusters that will boost your website's authority and rankings. Always share new posts on social media and via your Google Business Profile.

Guest blogging

As well as writing blog posts for your own site, you can also guest post for other, related sites. These guest posts can be a valuable source of backlinks and referral traffic if they appear on relevant blogs. Consider whether there are any martial arts websites that accept guest posts and contact them with a pitch for a topic you'd like to write about. If they accept your idea, most sites should be happy to include a backlink to your site along with an author bio.

Research blogs in your local area. You may find community blogs that focus on things to do in your town, for kids or adults, or that showcase local businesses. Backlinks from local sites such as these are valuable signals for the local search algorithms.

AI and content writing

If you are not a confident writer or have limited time, consider using an artificial intelligence tool to help you. With the advent of OpenAI's free ChatGPT software in late 2022 and the even more sophisticated models that followed, AI content writing has gone mainstream. Using written prompts, you can ask these tools to write a blog post for you on a given topic, although I would caution against relying on them too much. There is still no substitute for original insights written by a human, in your own tone of voice. AI-written content is easy to spot and will not contain any uniqueness or originality.

Instead, try using AI tools as a creative assistant. For example, you could ask one to "give me a list of blog post titles about the importance of nutrition in martial arts". AI tools are great for prompting ideas and speeding up certain tasks such as writing a post's metadata or providing an article's outline structure. Just don't let them do all the work, or content quality will suffer.

Video

Video marketing often goes hand in hand with social media, but YouTube videos can also play a part in your SEO strategy. You'll need at least some basic skills in filming and editing slick, informative video, but you don't need expensive kit.

Modern smartphones will do a pretty good job. Video topics can mirror those of your blog. In fact, you may choose to shoot a video first, then take the transcript and repurpose it as a blog post. You can also embed the YouTube video on the page for good measure.

When uploading to YouTube, think about appropriate keywords to enter, and to use in the video's title and description. Use the description to incorporate links back to your website. This may drive some traffic from users surfing YouTube itself, but Google sometimes shows YouTube videos in the organic results too. This can be a sneaky way to leapfrog your competitors and reach the top of the SERPs if your website isn't quite cutting it.

Video embedded within your website can increase your dwell time and engagement rate metrics. This makes your page appear more popular, and it may receive a slight boost in the algorithms.

Social media and SEO

Social media and SEO have a complicated relationship. There is disagreement in the industry over just how important social signals are for SEO. Social signals include posts with backlinks, likes, shares, and comments. These interactions don't have a direct impact on your search rankings, but we know that search engines pay some attention to social profiles. Remember E-E-A-T? It is likely that Google uses a brand's presence and reputation on social media to help understand its authority and expertise.

Visitors from social media are often more engaged than the average website visitor. Driving social traffic to your website can help to improve your average engagement rate and other on-site metrics. This can have an indirect positive influence on search rankings. Sharing your content widely on social media will increase the likelihood of other, authoritative brands mentioning you, which in turn improves your own brand's authority. By making your content as visible as possible on multiple platforms as well as just search engines, your chances of obtaining backlinks also go up. Having a strong social media presence as part of your broader marketing mix, creates a virtuous circle that feeds into your SEO.

Link all your social media profiles to your website, and vice versa. On your website, you can use the header or footer to include links to each social profile, allowing interested users to check out your social content. Also, try to maintain a regular posting schedule for each platform. It is much better to do one or two social channels well than to spread your resources too thin and come across as unengaging.

Use your content marketing approach to generate blogs and videos that will feed your social media schedule. Active feeds with good engagement could help your reputation on organic search. The goal is to dominate local search results for your target keywords, and social profiles can bolster your brand keyword performance. Social profiles also often rank high for searches on company names. By having a LinkedIn, Facebook, and Instagram account, you have more opportunities to rank for users searching on your name. In taking up more search result positions, you push your competitors down the rankings. Combining an optimised website with social media profiles and listing citations provides the best chance of a total page one lockout.

Linking social profiles

It is important for SEO purposes to cross-link your social media properties with your website. Every page on your site should contain a link to each social profile. You can add a row of social icons to the site header (above the menu) or to the footer. I recommend placing them in the footer, as they are secondary information and should not distract from your most important web pages.

Each social profile should include a link back to your website domain and, if possible, to your other social profiles. For example, by filling out all the fields on a Facebook page, you can add website and Instagram links. On Instagram, include your domain name in the bio, or use a service such as Linktree[14] to include a list of your important links. It is also a good idea to set up a profile with your business name on the most popular social media platforms and add a link to your web domain from the bio. It gives you an extra backlink and prevents anyone else from taking the name. Do this for Facebook, Instagram, Twitter, LinkedIn, YouTube and TikTok.

Fill out the "about us" or bio section of each social site so they are all consistent with each other, saying exactly who you are and what you offer. This can help you take over more of the top results in Google for searches on your brand name. Rather than just having your website in the top organic position and in the Local Pack, you can rank in extra positions with your

---

[14]https://linktr.ee

YouTube, LinkedIn, and Instagram pages, as well as the business listings discussed earlier.

Content marketing

You most likely won't have the time, expertise, or inclination to use every available channel and do it justice. It is much better to choose a few content channels and do them well than spread yourself too thin, failing to engage an audience meaningfully on any of them.

If you hate being in front of the camera, you may want to either focus on written content, or find someone else in your team who is more comfortable appearing in videos. For SEO, blogging is the single most effective channel, as the content is text-based, easy for search engines to index, and sits on your website rather than third-party platforms. But for maximum impact, a combination of website, video and social content will help grow your brand and raise awareness of your school.

Repurpose your content

Rather than create brand-new, unique content for each channel, save yourself time and energy by repurposing the same piece of content for various formats. For example, if you shoot a video on a topic, get the audio transcribed and use that as the basis of a blog post. Then, embed the original video into the blog post, to give your audience the choice over how to consume it. If you've written a "listicle" blog post, such as "the top ten ways to….", then you can turn this into an infographic and share it on your social accounts. There are various low-cost online tools for making infographics, including Canva.

Action Points

- ☐ Choose your favoured content channels and types.
- ☐ Conduct keyword research for your content ideas.
- ☐ Develop a content calendar.
- ☐ Link website and social profiles to each other.
- ☐ Get creating.
- ☐ Repurpose content for other channels.

13

TECHNICALLY SPEAKING...

Technical SEO factors, and how to run a technical audit.

As the name suggests, technical SEO focusses on the underlying aspects of your site relating to your code, content management system, server performance etc, rather than the words on the page. Technical aspects tend not to be so visible to users, but issues here can impede search engine spiders from correctly indexing your site. Technical SEO aims to make your website as easy to crawl as possible. It can be a vast subject, but here we will look at the most important factors you or your web developer should be aware of, to give your website the best possible chance of ranking.

Robots.txt

The robots.txt is a humble text file that lives in the root folder of your website. Its job is to tell search engine bots which folders they should crawl, and which they should avoid. You can use the robots.txt file to hide certain areas of your site from search engines, for example, your admin area, login page or members' area. It should also contain a link to your sitemap.

The robots.txt file can also block search engines from crawling other resources such as PDF downloads that you may not want to appear in search results.

Here's an example of a simple robots.txt:

```
User-Agent: *
Allow: /
Sitemap: https://www.yourdomain.com/sitemap.xml
```

This file tells all search engine crawlers that they can crawl the entire website, and where to find the sitemap.

To block search engines from indexing specific folders, use a "disallow" statement, followed by the sub-folder you want to block:

```
User-agent *
Disallow: /wp-admin
Disallow: /members-area
Sitemap: https://www.yourdomain.com/sitemap.xml
```

You can test the validity of your robots.txt file with Google's robots.txt Tester tool[15] or use one of the several free generators online to create one from scratch.

Site security

Having a secure website used to be an optional extra, but these days is an important ranking factor. Check that you have an SSL certificate installed for your domain, and that the http:// versions of your pages redirect to their https://

---

[15] https://www.google.com/webmasters/tools/robots-testing-tool

equivalents. If they do not, this could cause duplicate content issues. Set your SSL certificate to auto-renew via your web hosting provider or set a diary notification to remind you to renew it.

Sitemap

The sitemap is an xml file, usually called sitemap.xml or sitemap_index.xml, which lives in your site's root folder. It contains links to all your pages and posts. Sitemaps are important for search engines as their crawler bots can use the sitemap to identify URLs to crawl, and the logical hierarchy of a site. Most WordPress SEO plugins such as Yoast will generate a sitemap file for you. Check you have one by typing your domain name into the browser address bar, then adding /sitemap.xml at the end. Browse through it to ensure all pages that you want indexed are present. Then log into Google Search Console and submit the sitemap URL via the Indexing > Sitemaps screen if it is not already listed.

URL structure

When considering your website's structure, it is important to group pages logically together whilst avoiding a hierarchy that is too narrow and deep. A narrow and deep site is where there are lots of nested sub-folders, with important pages several folders away from the root. At the other extreme, it is best to avoid a shallow, unstructured site where most of the pages live in the root folder. This lack of structure makes it difficult for search engines to interpret how your pages relate to each other.

Plotting your pages and URLs in a spreadsheet can help you review your page hierarchy. Check for any pages with non-descriptive URLs or that do not contain appropriate keywords for the page. It is best to avoid sweeping changes to your page URLs, as this may harm your SEO. To minimise the risk of this, set up 301 permanent redirects from the old URL to the new one, if you do have to change any. This ensures that any links to those pages elsewhere in your website, or from other websites do not break, and preserves most of the page's link equity.

Site speed

We have looked at site speed elsewhere in this book, but checking how fast your website loads is an integral part of any technical SEO audit. Check for fast load times on desktop and mobile devices and aim to pass Google's Core Web Vitals tests. You can check your website's speed and Core Web vitals performance using PageSpeed Insights[16].

Redirect chains

A redirect chain is a situation where a redirect (a 301 permanent or 302 temporary redirect if you want to get technical) links to another redirect. It is possible for URLs to point to redirects, which are then themselves redirected, and so on. Redirect chains can arise over time as websites evolve. If a page becomes out of date, a website manager may remove it and redirect the link to another page. If the same thing then happens in turn to the target page, you have a redirect chain.

---

[16] pagespeed.web.dev

Redirect chains are bad because they slow down your page load and prevent crawlers from being able to access them. The slower load speed annoys users and consumes a search engine bot's crawl budget. For large sites, this can prevent the full site from indexing as the bot has to navigate layers of redirects. Redirect chains also prevent link equity from flowing between pages, causing the target page to drop in the rankings.

Broken links

Try to avoid broken links at all costs, as they have a significant negative impact on visitors and search crawlers. Bots follow links as they navigate around a website. If a link doesn't work, it is possible the search engines may not crawl the destination page. It is also a sign of lack of care and attention and makes a site appear less professional. Broken links can have an adverse effect on your web metrics, as frustrated users get confused or give up. Use an audit tool to scan your site every few months for broken links, then work your way down the report and fix them.

Missing ALT text

Automated SEO audits will also flag up any images that are missing ALT text. Edit any page containing one of these images and add descriptive ALT text, including appropriate keywords for the page. This is a quick and easy fix that requires no technical know-how. All you need to do is add a brief description of what the image depicts, then republish the page it appears on. This is also good practice from an accessibility perspective, as screen reader software for the visually impaired use ALT text to describe images.

Mobile responsiveness

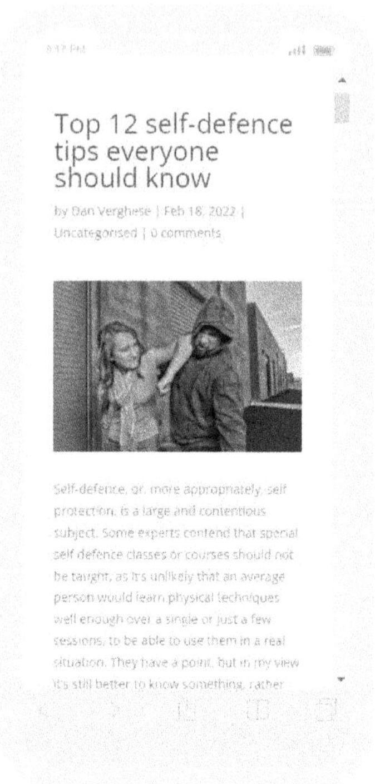

Check that all your pages load as expected on different form factors, e.g., laptop, tablet, and mobile phone. Google's index is now 'mobile first' so if your pages do not re-size and transform to a single-column layout or have annoying side-scrolling or embedded content using iframes, your mobile rankings may suffer. You can test your site's performance responsiveness using Google's Mobile-Friendly Test[17].

Duplicate content

Check your site for duplicate content, i.e. pages that contain exactly the same words as each other. An audit tool should flag this up. Either remove one of the offending pages or update them so the content is unique to that page. Duplicate content can confuse search engines and harm the ranking positions of affected pages.

Thin content

'Thin content' is a term denoting pages that have a very low word count. Google has no minimum word count, but pages that lack detail will not be comprehensive and lack value for readers. As a result, they will not rank high in search, and

[17] https://search.google.com/test/mobile-friendly

search engines may exclude them from their index. If you have pages with 300 words or fewer, consider removing, combining, or expanding them. Text-to-HTML ratio is also important here. If the page content doesn't justify the amount of HTML code behind the scenes, it may also not perform well. This can be a particular problem for sites that use front-end graphical page builders, like Divi or Elementor for WordPress. Page builders make a site easier for non-technical users to update, but suffer from 'code bloat', inserting many unnecessary HTML tags behind the scenes.

Duplicate metadata

Your technical audit should also identify any pages with duplicate meta descriptions or title tags. This can happen if you copy one page as the basis for another and forget to update the metadata. If you find any duplicates, update them so they are unique to and descriptive of the page.

Missing metadata

If any meta titles or descriptions are empty, fix these as you find them. Google will make up its own descriptions for its search results using content from the page itself, if it cannot find a good meta description. It may not pick the best content and the page's click through rate from the SERPs could suffer. Google sometimes replaces metadata anyway if it thinks it has found a better way to describe a page, but we want to avoid this where possible by writing clear and optimised metadata in the first place.

Non-indexed pages

Sometimes Google does not fully index your site, even if you have submitted a sitemap. Check for this on Search Console's Indexing > Pages screen. If any URLs are listed as "discovered – currently not indexed" or "crawled – currently not indexed", investigate why. You may need to update the page and then request a re-crawl from Google. This can occur for several reasons. Google may think that the page is not high enough quality or is a duplicate of another existing page. To encourage Google to index affected pages, try re-writing or expanding them, and adding more internal links from elsewhere on the site.

Schema markup

Schema markup, also called structured data, is a vocabulary of standardised tags added to a web page to describe its contents. Users do not see it, but tagging certain kinds of content with schema markup allows search engines to better understand it and provides richer features in search results.

The various SEO plugins available for WordPress allow you to tag pages with schema markup. For example, your FAQ or About Us pages can have specific markup added to tell search engines what they are. For online stores, schema markup on product pages allows Google to display the price and star ratings within search results. Ask your web developer to implement schema code based on Schema.org's Local Business category[18]. This category allows you to tag your contact details, address, opening hours, reviews, etc.

---

[18] https://schema.org/LocalBusiness

Having your website marked up with structured data will not make your pages rank higher. However, it increases the chances of you gaining "featured snippets" in the results pages. It can also improve click-through rates via more eye-catching and informative listings in the SERPs.

Canonicals

Canonical tags are simple HTML tags which, when added to the <head> section of a page's HTML code, denote the "main" version of a page. This is useful where you have duplicate pages with identical or very similar content. Google dislikes duplicate content and will only index one version of two identical pages. It must guess which version is the primary, or "canonical" one, unless you give it a clue. Canonical tags exist to tell Google which version it should include in the index and pass link equity to.

Duplicate pages can arise if a website administrator does not implement HTTPS redirects correctly, so it is good practice to check that any HTTP:// version of a page automatically re-directs to the HTTPS:// equivalent. If it does not, your web server's settings will need to be updated to correct this. They can also arise on pages which have a query string following them, for example, due to search results or product filters appending search query data to a page URL. In these cases, there is only a single page, but due to how Google spiders websites, it will interpret them as separate pages. To fix the problem, add:
<link rel="canonical" href="https://yourdomain.com/page-name/" /> to each page, replacing the URL with that of the page in question. This is a self-referring canonical tag that identifies the master version of the page for search engines.

Conducting SEO audits

It is good practice to audit your website from time to time, to identify any technical or content issues that may detract from your ability to rank. Larger sites or those that are updated with new content regularly should be audited more often than a site that rarely changes, as there are more opportunities for issues to creep in.

There are many tools on the market that will run a technical audit for you. Semrush and Ahrefs are the two most popular all-in-one SEO software suites, but they come at a price. Of course, you could subscribe for a month, run the audit, export the results, then cancel your subscription if you want to leverage the power of these tools without busting your budget.

A great alternative to this is the Screaming Frog SEO Spider. It is a freemium tool that allows you to crawl up to five hundred pages at a time before needing to pay, which is plenty for any martial arts school website. It is a little less intuitive though and feels more "techie" than Semrush and Ahrefs, but is a powerful and useful tool.

Regular, or at least occasional audits are a good way to systematise your SEO and mop up any problems that have crept into your site.

Download the free Technical SEO Audit Template that accompanies this book at **https://bit.ly/seo-dojo-download**

Action Points

- ☐ Run a technical audit using SEO software.
- ☐ Audit and optimise metadata.
- ☐ Check sitemap files and the robots.txt.
- ☐ Check Search Console for indexing errors.
- ☐ Ensure canonical tags are correct.
- ☐ Use local schema markup.

14

MEASURE YOUR WAY TO SUCCESS

The wonderful world of website analytics.

You've audited your website, rewritten your pages and metadata, optimised your on-page SEO and built your first backlinks. But how do you know if your efforts are paying off? SEO is often a case of trial-and-error, and optimisation decisions should be based on data. Fortunately, website performance is very measurable, and you can monitor your traffic and user behaviour in almost real-time.

Google Analytics

Google Analytics (GA) is the ubiquitous analytics software in use on most websites these days. Google Analytics 4 is free, and relatively straightforward to set up. If your site runs on WordPress, there are a variety of plugins available to simplify this process even further for you.

If you do not have GA running already, sign up for a free account, enter your domain name and complete the setup wizard. Then either take the tracking code and embed it onto every page of your website or copy your tracking ID number and add it to your website analytics plugin. It is best to use a plugin or add the code to your theme's header. If you are more tech-savvy, you can add the tracking code via Google Tag Manager instead. Once GA is in place, load your website in a browser window and then look at the Real-Time analytics screen to check that your session is being tracked.

Google Analytics provides many useful reports. To zero-in on the effect your SEO is having on your site, look at the Traffic Acquisition report. This tells you how much of your web traffic has come from each acquisition channel, for example organic, referral, direct, or social. Traffic from search engine results is "organic", whereas traffic via backlinks is reported under "referral". Check in every month to see whether your traffic is going up or down, how this compares to the previous month or the previous year, and what contribution organic is making to the total.

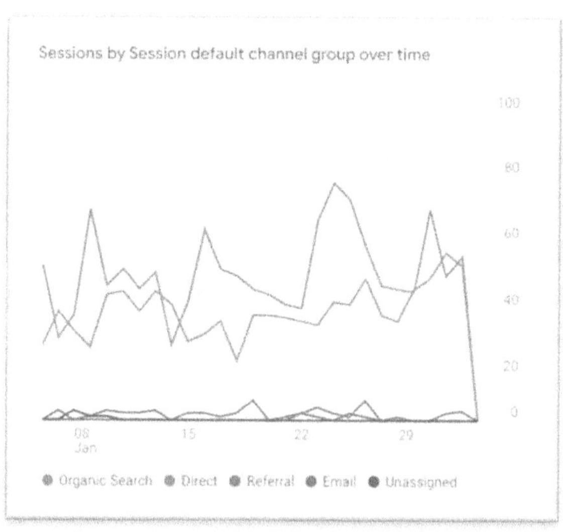

Google Analytics 4 default channel grouping report

If you notice spikes or dips in your report, think about whether these correlate to any major changes you made on your website. Once you make a change, it will take some time for search engines to pick them up and factor them into their algorithms. This depends on how often their spiders re-crawl your site, which could be anything from a few days to a few weeks.

The Landing Page report in GA's engagement reports will tell you which pages on your website are attracting the most traffic. This will help you understand where most user journeys begin and help you optimise further. You'll be able to see whether most of your visitors are arriving at the home page or going to one of your sub-pages. As your search engine optimisation of your programme/service or location pages bears fruit, you'll see more visitors arriving directly on these pages rather than your homepage.

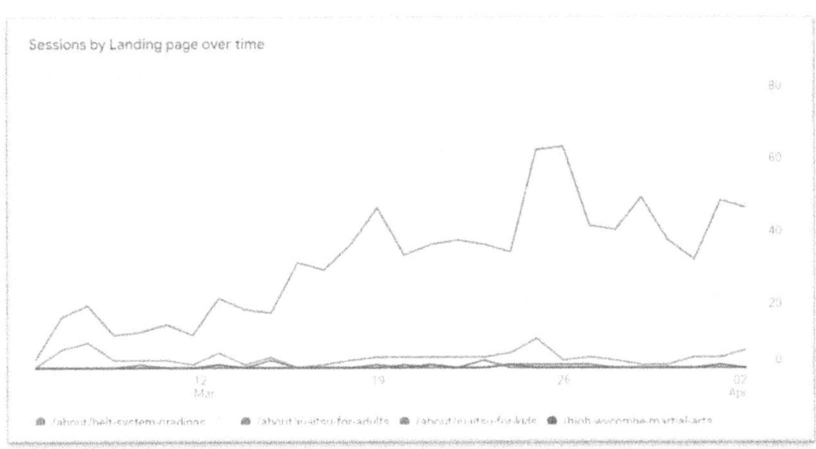

Google Analytics 4 default landing pages report

On-site metrics

Google Analytics is a sophisticated and powerful tool, but which metrics of the many available should you pay attention to? The metrics below are those used in Google Analytics 4.

Metric	**What does it mean?**
Users	The total number of active users.
New users	Users for which this was their first visit during the selected period.
Sessions	The total number of sessions (a user may visit more than once, so the session count is likely to be higher than the user count).
Engaged sessions	Sessions where the user interacted with your website somehow or stayed longer than 10 seconds.
Average engagement time	The average time users interacted with your website.
Session by default channel grouping	To measure your SEO's effectiveness, look at how many sessions are being contributed by the Organic Search metric, within the "default channel grouping" dimension.
Sessions by landing page	Look at this to see which pages your users are arriving on the site at, to see which are performing well and which are failing to attract traffic.

Conversion Rate	The conversion rate is the percentage of all users who perform a conversion on a site. Conversions (called Conversion Events in Google Analytics 4) are user actions on your site that you regard as particularly important and that may lead to new leads or sales. Other "micro-conversions" are also important, e.g. brochure downloads, newsletter sign-ups. You can set these conversions up in Google Analytics and track them. Try to build landing pages to maximise your conversion rate as much as possible.

An in-depth guide to configuring Google Analytics is beyond the scope of this book, but Google provides free online training via their Skillshop site[19].

Search engine results position tracking

As well as monitoring your on-site traffic, put a system in place for tracking where your website ranks for your target keywords. There are lots of paid tools that will do this for you, but they are not worth spending money on for small, local business sites. Instead, I recommend using a simple spreadsheet.

Plot your list of target keywords down each row of the first column, then the months of the year in each of the next

[19] https://skillshop.exceedlms.com

columns. Then, duplicate the tab so you end up with one table for desktop results, and another tab for mobile. Most of your traffic will be from mobile devices, so these rankings are most important, but it can be worth tracking both.

To populate your results, open a web browser in your laptop or mobile phone (depending on which tab you're starting with). Use incognito or private browsing mode, and do not log into your Google account. This will give you more reliable results than a standard logged-in browser window, as your past search behaviour cannot influence the results. Now search for each keyword one by one and scan down the results until you find one of your pages listed. Note its position in the spreadsheet. If your site appears in the Local Pack above the organic results, note this too. For example, if my website ranks in second place on the Local Pack but is also in position six of page one, I enter "LP2, 6" in the appropriate cell.

You may also want to take note of which pages are ranking, as different ones will likely appear for different keywords. Sometimes your home page will rank first, on other occasions it is likely to be a programme or location landing page. I only check the first three pages of Google results when I do this. Anything further takes too long and will not yield any traffic anyway. For all future months I colour-code the cells according to whether the position has improved (green), fallen (red) or stayed the same (grey), relative to the preceding month. Set a reminder in your calendar to repeat this process and update the spreadsheet during the first week of each month. It should take no longer than an hour. If it does, you are tracking too many keywords. Don't overcomplicate things - keep the number of keywords to twenty or fewer.

To download the ready-made, free tracking template that accompanies this book, visit:

https://bit.ly/seo-dojo-download

Action Points

- ☐ Create a Google Analytics account.
- ☐ Embed the tracking code on your website.
- ☐ Familiarise yourself with the basic GA4 reports.
- ☐ Track your position in the SERPs each month.

APPENDICES

APPENDIX I

SEO TOOLS

The market is full of software designed to help you improve your SEO, and they can be a fantastic help, if you know how to use them and have the budget. In an ideal world, it is always best to make decisions based on real data rather than on a hunch. Many of these tools aggregate vast amounts of search data to help guide your keyword research and SEO plan.

Martial arts school owners have modest marketing budgets and lack the time or specialist knowledge needed to make agency-grade sophisticated tools worthwhile. To get started, you don't need to spend any money. All you need is:

- Google Search
- Google Search Console
- Google Keyword Planner (part of Google Ads)
- Google Sheets (for tracking your keywords and rankings)
- A free speed-testing site
- Your brain.

The list of other tools below is not exhaustive, but I have included tools that I either use personally or that have an excellent reputation in the SEO industry. Some have free tiers, or time-limited free trials.

Analytics

Campaign URL Builder - https://ga-dev-tools.google/campaign-url-builder/

Google Analytics - https://analytics.google.com/analytics/web

Google Search Console - https://search.google.com/search-console

Hotjar - www.hotjar.com

Looker Studio (used to be called Google Data Studio) - https://datastudio.google.com

Backlinks

Ahrefs Backlink Checker - https://ahrefs.com/backlink-checker

Keyword research

Answer The Public - www.answerthepublic.com

Google Keyword Planner - https://ads.google.com/intl/en_uk/home/tools/keyword-planner

Google Trends - trends.google.com/trends

KWFinder - www.kwfinder.com

Moz Keyword Explorer - moz.com/explorer

Ubersuggest - https://neilpatel.com/ubersuggest

Chrome browser extensions

Ahrefs SEO Toolbar - ahrefs.com/seo-toolbar

GMB Everywhere - https://www.gmbeverywhere.com

Keywords Everywhere - https://keywordseverywhere.com

MozBar - moz.com/products/pro/seo-toolbar

SEO Minion - seominion.com

SEO Quake - seoquake.com

Local SEO

BrightLocal - www.brightlocal.com

Google Business Profile - www.google.com/intl/en_uk/business

LocalFalcon - www.localfalcon.com

Site audit

Screaming Frog - https://www.screamingfrog.co.uk/seo-spider

Premium all-in-one SEO tools

Ahrefs - www.ahrefs.com

Semrush - www.semrush.com

Content creation

ChatGPT – https://chat.openai.com

Frase – www.frase.io

Grammarly - www.grammarly.com

Hemingway - hemingwayapp.com

SurferSEO - surferseo.com

Website speed test

GTmetrix - https://gtmetrix.com

PageSpeed Insights - https://pagespeed.web.dev

Pingdom - www.pingdom.com

APPENDIX II

SEO LEARNING RESOURCES

The Internet is awash with resources for both amateur and professional SEOs. Much of it is contradictory, out of date, or impenetrable to the average business owner. It is difficult to know where to start and how to separate the wheat from the chaff. These recommended resources will help you keep up to date with the ever-evolving world of search engine optimisation.

Free online courses & certifications

Google Skillshop - https://skillshop.withgoogle.com
(Check out the Google Analytics courses and certifications)

Hubspot Academy SEO Certification Course - https://academy.hubspot.com/courses/seo-training

Semrush Academy - www.semrush.com/academy

Ahrefs Academy - https://ahrefs.com/academy
(I particularly recommend the Blogging for Business course)

Yoast's SEO for Beginners training - https://yoast.com/academy/free-seo-training-seo-for-beginners

Websites & blogs

Ahrefs Blog - https://ahrefs.com/blog

Google Search Central Blog - developers.google.com/search/blog (for official updates straight from the horse's mouth)

Moz Blog - /moz.com/blog

Reddit - www.reddit.com/r/techseo
www.reddit.com/r/bigseo

Search Engine Journal - www.searchenginejournal.com

Search Engine Land - searchengineland.com

Semrush Blog - www.semrush.com/blog

Yoast SEO Blog - yoast.com/seo-blog

APPENDIX III

RECOMMENDED READING

SEO books

Roger Bryan, *Local SEO Secrets: 20 Local SEO Strategies you Should Be Using Now*

Will Coombe, *3 Months to No.1: The "No-Nonsense" SEO Playbook For Getting Your Website Found on Google*

Martial arts business books

Buzz Durkin, Success Is Waiting: The Martial Arts School Owner's Guide To Teaching, Business, and Life

Cristina Rodriguez, *The Best Known Dojo: A Marketing Book for Martial Arts School Owners*

Gordon Burcham, *The Business Of Martial Arts*

Mike Massie, *Small Dojo Big Profits*

Paul Halme, *How To Make Money With Your Martial Arts Gym: Even If You Haven't Won Anything Yet*

APPENDIX IV

GLOSSARY OF TERMS

Term	Definition
301 redirect	A method of sending web traffic from one URL automatically to another. 301 redirects are 'permanent', and transfer some of the original page's link equity to the new destination.
302 redirect	A method of sending web traffic from one URL automatically to another. 302 redirects are 'temporary', and do not lead to search engines transferring the link equity of the original, redirected page to the new one.
404 error	A status code meaning that the requested page cannot be found on the server, perhaps because the hyperlink is incorrect, or the page no longer exists.
Above the fold	A marketing term dating back to newspapers, referring to the words that appeared in the top half of the page, visible before the reader unfolds the paper. In digital marketing, it refers to website content that the user can see without having to scroll.
Algorithm	Process or set of rules used by search engines to determine what results to show for a specific search, and in what order. Algorithms look at and weight many

	'ranking factors' to decide on how they will order their results.
ALT text	An HTML attribute of the IMG tag which describes the contents of an image for search engines and visually impaired users.
Anchor text	The words used in a hyperlinked piece of text.
Backlink / link	A hyperlink from a third-party website to your business site. Backlinks come in two SEO 'flavours': no-follow and do-follow.
Black hat	SEO techniques that try to fool search engines through practises that contravene search engines' guidelines. Black hat SEO can lead to sites being penalised and de-ranked, if they get caught.
Bounce rate	A metric which measures the percentage of website users who leave a site after visiting one page and not interacting any further with the site, as if they were 'bouncing off' a window.
Call to Action (CTA)	An instruction to a website user to take a specific action on the page, e.g. 'download' or 'call us now'.
Canonical tag	An HTML tag (rel="canonical") that identifies the main, definitive version of a web page for search engines, where several identical or near-identical versions of a page exist.

Citation	A mention of your business online on a third-party website.
Click-Through Rate (CTR)	A metric showing the percentage of users who click through to a website from the search engine results page.
Content Delivery Network (CDN)	A cloud-based distributed network of servers providing worldwide caching for websites, to improve load times regardless of the visitor's location.
Content Management System (CMS)	Software used to create and manage the pages and other content of a website, as opposed to hard coding all pages. Popular content management systems include WordPress, Squarespace, Wix, Joomla, Drupal, Squarespace, Shopify, etc.
Conversion	An important action you want a user to take on a web page. For example, filling in a contact form, calling the business, or making a purchase.
Conversion Rate (CR)	A metric showing users who have converted as a percentage of total users.
Crawl budget	The number of pages a search engine's bot will crawl each time it visits your site.
CSS	Cascading Style Sheets. Code used on websites to set the visual style and positioning of elements on a page.
Do-follow link	A normal backlink from one website to another, that a search engine bot can crawl.

E-E-A-T	Experience - Expertise - Authoritativeness - Trustworthiness. A fundamental component of Google's search quality rater guidelines, used to evaluate the effectiveness of search results against user requirements.
Googlebot	The name of Google's programme that crawls the Internet, following links from page to page and site to site, to build up and refresh Google's index of the web. Googlebot is a type of spider/bot/crawler.
Header Tag	An HTML tag used to wrap around heading or subheading text, e.g. <h1>This is a heading</h1>. There are six levels of header tag in HTML.
Heatmap	A visual representation of user engagement with a website, showing where they have clicked or moved their pointers.
Help A Reporter Out (HARO)	A service for journalists to connect with subject matter experts and obtain quotes and information to use in their articles.
HTML	Hyper-Text Markup Language. The specific type of markup used on web pages to describe and structure the information on them.
Index / Indexing	The index is a search engine's database of all the web pages it knows about. Search engine 'spiders', or bots, index websites by following links from page to page. Googlebot indexes websites for Google and adds their pages to its database.

Keyword	A single or multi-word phrase typed by a user into a search engine.
Keyword stuffing	The outdated SEO practice of over-using keywords on a page in the hope of positively influencing search results.
Landing page	Either a stand-alone page or other page within a website that visitors are likely to enter the site, or 'land', on.
Link equity (also colloquially 'link juice')	The value passed by a backlink to the linked web page, determined via a search engine's algorithm.
Local Pack (also 3-Pack or Map Pack)	The first few local results, often displayed at the top of Google's Page 1 local search results. Includes a Google map and other info, such as star ratings/reviews.
Local SEO	The sub-discipline of SEO concerned with ranking web sites as prominently as possible for searchers in a specific geographic area.
Long-tail keyword	A more specific keyword, comprising three or more words. As they are more specific, they have lower search volume than short-tail keywords, but usually have higher purchase intent. Usually easier to rank for than short-tail keywords.
Manual action	A penalty imposed by Google's human reviewers on a website for breaching its webmaster quality guidelines, which negatively affects search rankings.

Meta description	A short snippet of text describing what a page is about, stored in the page's HTML.
Meta tags	HTML tags that hold data which describes a web page. Used by search engines and web browser software, among others.
Meta title	The title of the page, held in an HTML tag and displayed by search engines, browser tabs and social media sites.
NAP	**N**ame, **A**ddress and **P**hone number.
No-follow link	A hyperlink with the "rel=nofollow" attribute applied to their HTML tag. This tells search engine spiders not to follow the link.
Off-page SEO	Optimisation techniques focussing on influencing other sites to provide backlinks or citations.
On-page SEO	Optimisation techniques focussing on improving the website/web pages themselves, to improve rankings. Can include technical aspects or content optimisation.
Organic traffic	Visitors arriving to a website from search engine results (as opposed to paid, social media or direct traffic).
Organic results	Search engine results that are unpaid, i.e., not resulting from PPC ads.
Position	The place in the search engine results that a web page appears in, for a specific search term.

Ranking factor	Information that a search engine includes in the mathematical algorithm it uses to calculate and display search results. Ranking factors include backlinks, content relevance, and metadata. Google uses over 200 ranking factors in its algorithm.
Reciprocal link	Two web sites or domains that link to each other.
Redirect	Where one URL is re-routed to another, possibly due to older content being removed or the website re-structured. See 301 redirect and 302 redirect.
Schema markup	A type of website markup code that describes specific types of information on a page, to provide context and understanding to search engines. Also called 'structured data'.
SEO	Search engine optimisation.
SERPs	Search engine results pages.
Short-tail keyword	A search phrase, usually made up of one or two words. They have high volume but usually lower purchase intent and are harder to rank for than long-tail keywords.
Sitemap	An XML file that lists out all crawlable pages on a website and sits within the root folder.
Spider	Computer programmes used by search engines that crawl the web, following links and sitemaps to 'index' a site. Also called 'bots', 'robots' or 'crawlers'.

Technical SEO	The sub-discipline of SEO that is concerned with removing any technical issues with the website or hosting that may negatively affect rankings or prevent pages from being fully indexed, as opposed to addressing the visible content.
Topical authority	An SEO concept whereby a business demonstrates deep expertise and authority on a specific topic through the publication of quality content, to positively influence its search engine positions. SEO professionals create interlinked 'content clusters' to build up authority around a topic area.
URL	Uniform Resource Locator, otherwise known as a website address. Every web page has its own unique URL, displayed in the browser address bar.
White hat	SEO techniques that are legitimate and do not contravene search engines' terms of service or guidelines.

FREE DOWNLOADS

Don't forget to download the free resources that accompany this book, so you can get started and save time on your SEO campaign.

You'll have access to my:

- Technical SEO Audit Template
- On-Page SEO Audit Template
- Keyword Position Tracking Template.

Visit https://bit.ly/seo-dojo-download

Or scan the QR code below:

NEED HELP?

If you think all this SEO business sounds like too much hard work and you'd like it done for you, or if you need training or advice, please get in touch to discuss your needs.

I'm a freelance Digital Marketing Consultant with over 20 years' experience, and can help you with:

- SEO strategy and implementation
- Digital marketing strategy and advice
- Email marketing and automation
- Web content and copywriting
- Digital marketing training.

I'm also available for speaking engagements and events.

Email: info@dan-verghese.digital

Web: www.dan-verghese.digital

LinkedIn: www.linkedin.com/in/danielverghese

INDEX

G

H

I

J

K

L

M

N

ALSO BY DAN VERGHESE

Essential Ju-Jitsu

Origins, Principles & Practices

Available from Amazon in Paperback, Hardcover and Ebook.

ABOUT THE AUTHOR

Dan Verghese began training in martial arts at the age of seventeen and holds a second dan black belt in taekwondo, and a third dan black belt in traditional ju-jitsu. He has also trained in bojutsu, kobudo, eskrima, judo, Brazilian jiu-jitsu and aikido. He has taught martial arts professionally, operating his own school that achieved a 130% year-on-year growth in student numbers.

Dan has over twenty years' experience delivering and managing high-performing websites and campaigns, having managed digital marketing teams at start-ups, FTSE 100 companies and SEO agencies. He also works as a mentor and assessor to students on digital marketing training and certification programmes.

Dan specialises in SEO, web project management, content writing and email marketing, offering freelance consulting to the martial arts, wellness and professional education sectors.

His first book, *Essential Ju-Jitsu: Origins, Principles & Practices* was published in 2022.

www.dan-verghese.digital

www.ingramcontent.com/pod-product-compliance
Ingram Content Group UK Ltd.
Pitfield, Milton Keynes, MK11 3LW, UK
UKHW020142250726
13967UKWH00002B/824

9 781739 426804